The History
of New Quay
in 12 Tales

Kathleen Fawle

First published in the UK and Ireland 2023 by Kathleen.Fawle

Kathleen Fawle can be contacted at Kathleen.fawle33@gmail.com

A catalogue record for this book is available from the British Library.

Front cover image Finavarra House from Skerrett Estate papers used with permission of Emma Barrett.
Formatting, interior design, and cover design by Woven Red Author Services

ISBN: 978-1-7394718-0-4 (Print version)
ISBN: 978-1-7394718-1-1 (eBook version)

Table of Contents

List of Illustrations

List of Tables

Introduction

New Quay, at the edge of the Burren, lying on the south coast of Galway Bay, attracts thousands of tourists. For many of these tourists it serves as a scenic stop off point on their journey along the Wild Atlantic Way. Many of those visitors will look at the landscape, ancient monuments, ruins of big houses and wonder about the stories behind them. Every hill, church ruin, old house and shoreline holds secrets, secrets of the lives of the people who lived, loved, laboured, traded, fished, prayed, emigrated, or died there. Most left no mark, their lives having faded into oblivion, much of history now forgotten. History can be distorted. In a deeply hierarchical society, the majority of those who left contemporary records were members of the privileged minority, while the poor and less well-off left little behind. Even the newspapers of the day, owned by the rich and powerful, provided descriptions of events and happening coloured by the agenda of their patrons.

The history of New Quay is rich in mystery and intrigue. People have been coming here for thousands of years, from hunter gatherers who left no trace, followed by the first farmers 5000 years ago. The farmers climbed up Turlough Hill and built temporary homes, a colossal stone fort and cairns for their dead long before the Egyptians planned the great pyramids at Giza. Why they came, what strange rituals they performed, the gods they petitioned and why they chose such an exposed place are enigmas that continues to intrigue 5000 years later.

Early Christian hermits from the 6th century AD, St Colman McDuagh being the most notable, were drawn here. In search of peace and quiet, St Colman, having served his time as Bishop of Kilmacduagh, sought a remote place where he could be alone with his god, choosing Oughtmama to end his days as his final resting place. Monks, successors to St Colman, coveted the life he had built here and continued to make their homes in this sacred place for well-nigh a thousand years.

The next monastic community that left its mark was that of the Cistercians. For eight hundred years, the architectural remains and unique stonework of the abbey they built, Corcomroe, has continued to captivate. Arriving at the end of the 12th or early 13th century, the Cistercians came at the invitation of the O'Briens kings of Munster. The early history of the abbey is interwoven with the history of the O'Briens and their struggles to retain their domination over Thomond.

As well as seeking spiritual sanctuaries, those who came, included those who left their cultural marks on the landscape. Donnchadh O'Dalaigh, whose memorial stands near Parkmore Quay, was the first of a long line of O'Dalaigh poets to make their home in Finavarra. He was described as the greatest poet since Ovid and is credited with setting up a bardic school, which in its heyday had over 150 students studying there.

The last quarter of the 19th century and early 20th saw the emergence of the Gaelic and Literary Revival. At the heart of the revival stood Lady Gregory and W.B. Yeats. Lady Gregory, who spent her childhood summers in Cartron

House, purchased Mount Vernon Lodge on the Flaggy Shore in 1912 as a holiday home for her only son Robert Gregory. The Gregory family spent summers there, entertaining many of Ireland's literary and artistic giants. But in her writings Lady Gregory also spoke of her gradual awakening to the world around her. She wrote of the influence of the people of the Burren, of her growing perception that folklore was an intrinsic part of their lives, as natural as the landscape and an inevitable result of its airy blueness; *"Shadows of cloud and rock by day and shadows of thoughts of dreams of the dead by night."*

The 19th century was also the period when the Flaggy Shore became a popular holiday destination for the gentry of Clare and South Galway. James Skerrett of Galway purchased the lands in Finavarra in the 1690s, from Carey Dillon, an adventurer who had been granted land in lieu of payment for his military support during the Cromwellian Wars. The Skerrett family were to retain the estate until the early 20th century. They built a string of lodges along the Flaggy Shore, renting them for the Summer to their 'fashionable visitors" whose arrival and departures were noted in the social columns of the newspapers.

But the story of New Quay is not just about the elite, the gentry who built fine houses and frolicked on the Flaggy Shore. The tenant farmers, trades people and the landless who made up over ninety nine percent of the population have left little record of their lives. But first-hand accounts can be gleaned from Government reports commissioned when it was obvious in the 19th century that the landlord system wasn't working. The 1835 Poor Law commission with evidence from New Quay and the Devon Commission report of 1843 with testimony from local landlord Burton Bindon, highlight the precipitous nature of the life of the poor in the pre famine era. The devastation caused by the failure of the potato crop and the ensuring famine can be gleaned from various reports in the newspapers of the day. The census summaries and the reports from the New Quay parish priest Reverend Coffey provide startling evidence of the dramatic drop in population numbers. The housing statistics in the census show more than half the population residing in one roomed cabins. Although it is less than 200 years since the famine, little evidence endures; the ruins of the fever hospital survive in Kinvara, the existence of a single wall remains of the workhouse in Ballyvaughan, but no mass graves for famine victims are evident in New Quay. The numerous houses existing on marginal land by roadside, mountains and sea have all disappeared without trace.

New Quay has endured centuries of occupation. It is seeded with stories of the past and my motivation in writing this book is to bring those stories to light. When the past is forgotten and lost it is important that we try to remember those who have gone before. Their lives may be a mystery. but oral tradition, newspapers from the eras, diaries, and government reports, although often biased in favour of the ruling elite, along with place names, allow us to unravel the past. My book tells the history of New Quay, its past, sometimes tempestuous, through the people and places that shaped it but also place it in the context of the wider world.

Section 1.
The Privileged
and the Poor

1. The Tale of the Skerretts of Finavarra House

Introduction

They are found all over Ireland, ruins of abandoned great houses and mansions, symbols of an elite society, the remnants of the lives of a privileged few from a bygone colonial era. Finavarra House is one such ruined mansion, situated in a prominent position overlooking Muckinish Bay, facing towards Ballyvaughan and the Burren Hills. For over 200 years it was the home of the Skerrett family, the family seat of their Finavarra and Burren estates. What remains today are the crumbling ruins of a large, detached L plan house. This, *"great house"* was built in the second half of the 18th century by Hyacinth Skerrett and reported to be the third house built on the site.

Wandering in the derelict ruins, through the house and outhouses, under the crumbling masonry, you may wonder about the people and the lives of those who once lived there and what happened to them. William Minor Skerrett and his wife Anna were the last family to oversee the estate in the second half of the 19th century. They had 14 children, including 10 sons. The *"harem scarem"* sons, described by their nephew in his biography as: *"Nimrods, big men, handsome men with charming manners, living hard, drinking hard, keen sportsmen who shot, fished, and hunted. They received a classical education, at the top Catholic schools in England and Ireland, so they could quote a line from Horace with the best and several of them took degrees from Trinity College."* But the 10 sons all died young, with all but one in their graves before the age of 50. The last one to die, Hyacinth, a Catholic priest, died aged 53 in 1900. Only one of the 10 had children, with just one male heir and that heir became a monk in a Belgian monastery, so the Finavarra Skerretts died out in the male line and their family name became extinct. The Skerrett family history in Ireland can be traced back to the 1200s and Ireland's history following the Anglo-Norman invasion.

Origins in Galway

The name Skerrett was derived from 'Huscared', and the Finavarra ancestors are believed to have come to Galway from England in the 1240's with Richard De Burgo. They were one of the 12 tribes of Galway but as well as being residents of the town of Galway, records showed that branches of the family held lands and estates in counties Mayo and Galway.

Between the 15th and 17th century, members of the 14 leading tribes or merchant families, who were mainly of Anglo-Norman descent, dominated the commercial, social, and political life of Galway. The term 'Tribes of Galway' was applied as a derogatory term by the Cromwellian officer who tried to negotiate with them and was frustrated by the close alliance between the merchants. However, it was a term the families used and retained as a badge of honour. The wealth and prosperity of Galway during these centuries was largely attributed to the trade networks which the merchants forged with France and Spain along the Atlantic seaboard. In the early 17th century before the Cromwellian wars, Galway port was described by the authorities in charge *"as the most considerable port of trade in the three kingdoms, second only to the port of London".*

Although they were staunchly Catholic, the merchant families managed to retain their power and influence throughout the Reformation (and the political and religious upheavals during the reigns of Henry, Elizabeth, and later monarchs). It may be that the English monarchs saw them as less of a threat and easier to deal with than the Gaelic chieftains who the merchants managed to keep at bay. The relationship between the merchant families and the native Gaelic families of Connaught was often difficult. Although there were times when they mixed and intermarried, and Irish became the main language of the town, there were also periods when the Gaelic natives were banished outside the city walls. *"That neither O ne Mac, should strutte ne swagger through the streets of Galway"* was one such byelaw according to Hardiman that was passed in 1518 to keep out the Gaelic natives from the town. The tribes' fear of the native chieftains is also reflected in an inscription over the west gate of the town that read; *"From the ferocious O'Flahertys, Good Lord deliver us."*

But while relations were sometimes hostile, when faced with the Cromwellian threat, both the natives and merchant families joined forces against the common enemy. From 1641 the English Parliamentary forces' civil war against Charles I led to a ruthless campaign in Ireland against what they saw as the Catholic perpetrators of an assault on the Protestant colonists. On the 20th of March 1652 Galway was the last stronghold to surrender to the military under Captain Ludlow.

Having surrendered, the merchant rulers of Galway initially appeared to secure good terms with the enemy. The terms agreed, permitted the former residents to keep most of their property. However very soon the new administration's excessive taxation rules made life difficult for the earlier inhabitants. It was said that a trumpet sounded each Saturday in the town and if the taxes were not immediately paid, the soldiers rushed in and seized the property of those who failed to pay up. Under new legislation in 1655, all Catholics were directed to leave town by the 30th of October. They were offered the equivalent cost of an 8-year lease of the purchase price of their property or else face confiscation. Many of the merchant families, Skerretts included, left the town, and invested the wealth they had accumulated as traders in purchasing estates in Clare and Connaught.

Origins in Finavarra

The first mention of the Skerretts' property in Finavarra is in the will of James Skerrett FitzMarcus, in 1691, who gave his profession as *"Merchant of the town of Galway"*. In his will he left to his eldest son, Anthony Skerrett, his estate in counties Galway and Roscommon that he had purchased from Colonel Legg. To his second son William Skerrett he left the estate in Tinavarra in Burren County Clare that he had recently purchased from Colonel Cary Dillon.

Like many of the new English transplanters Cary Dillon faced many difficulties. Captain Ludlow (Provisional Commander for the subjugation of Ireland from 1651) was notorious for the destruction and havoc he left in Ireland following his military campaign. County Clare was one of the places most severely impacted. Ludlow, in his rampage through the Burren famously remarked;

"The Burren affordeth not a piece of timber sufficient to hang a man, water in any one place to drown a man, or earth enough in any one part to bury him and yet their cattle are very fat; for the grass growing in turfs of earth, of two or three foot square, that lie

between the rocks, which are of limestone, is very sweet and nourishing."

The county was devastated, and many places were left as wilderness after Ludlow performed his worst excesses, destroying houses, castles, churches, animals, and crops in his wake to ensure the rebel forces could not retaliate. The population of Clare is believed to have dropped more than 20 per cent due to the slaughter and subsequent famine.

The transplanters faced with such devastation, were confronted with the tough task of rebuilding in a country they had little knowledge of. The British authorities acknowledged the threat of the three enemies, wolves, priests, and Tories. To rid the country of wolves, the new government offered a payment of £5 on proof, for each one killed. Priests were rounded up and prisons created for them on Inishbofin and Inishmore. The rebels, the Tories, faced death or deportation. It's ironic that the name Tory, (derived from the Irish word Toraigh for outlaw, robber or brigand and first used for those who secretly attacked the new settlers) has come to its current meaning in the British establishment for UK Conservative party members.

Faced with such a hostile environment, many of the adventurers sold the lands granted to them, to whoever would buy it and went home to England. Cary Dillon who had been granted the lands of Finavarra, sold, and disposed of them as he did with his other coastal properties. The land was sold back to either the dispossessed or other Irish settlers throughout the following years. It is reported that Skerretts paid £50 for the first lot of land in the townland of Rine next to Finavarra. Many of the lands in Ballyvaughan and Ballyvelaghan later came into the hands of the Skerretts. In the early 18th century, William Skerrett purchased lands in Ballyvaughan from the Stauntons and by the time of the land valuations of the mid 19th century, the family in Finavarra had in their name over 2600 acres in County Clare as well as a string of properties and lodges along the Flaggy Shore.

Skerrett Family in Finavarra

William Skerrett inherited the estate on the death of his father James in 1691 and was the first Skerrett to live in Finavarra. William Skerrett married Martha Kerwin of Dalgan, County Mayo. Together they had 5 children, Hyacinth, his heir, William, Mary, Margaret, and Catherine. In 1719 and again in 1756 William placed advertisements in Pue's Occurrences, offering a lease on his property in Finavarra. This is the 1756 detailed account of the estate.

> *"TO BE LET. from the first day of May next for such a term of years to be agreed upon, the lands of Finavarra containing 412 acres. Also the Lands Balygrenane alias Knocnageeha, containing 222 Acres, 3 Roods, 25 Perches, both lying and being in the Barony of Burren and County of Clare, being part of the Estate of William Skerrett, Esq. Lying within three Miles of each other, there are excellent sheep walks as any in the county for fattening and rearing, and remarkably good for tillage, having the sea weld all about it, and some of the land is very good for rearing black cattle. The said lands are delightfully situated by the seaside, in fine air and beautiful prospect. The area is well improved, with a good convenient Farmhouse' and Offices, a large young orchard in full bearing, and the lands are well enclosed by double stone walls, five and six Feet high. Proposals will be received by the said William Skerrett at his house at Finavarra aforesaid."*

During William's lifetime there were restrictions on Catholics owning property. To get round the Penal Laws many Catholics entered into agreements with those of the Established Church to lease their lands. When he died, William left the Finavarra estate to his eldest son Hyacinth.

Hyacinth Skerrett is listed as one of the people who converted from Catholicism to Protestantism in 1766. The family had always been Catholic as were subsequent generations. They were generous benefactors to the church and many members became priests and nuns and included a bishop amongst their number. Hyacinth's conversion to Protestantism was probably considered an expedient move in the times of the Penal Laws, when the restrictions upon Catholics buying land and property and holding office were prohibitive. To prove his conversion, Hyacinth would have had to denounce what the Protestant church, then the established church, called Popery. He would have sworn before a Protestant clergyman his disbelief in transubstantiation and praying to and adoration of Mary and the saints. Two years after his conversion, Hyacinth married in a Protestant church in Chester in England, his bride a wealthy heiress. The Chester Courant in 1768 announced the marriage.

"Last Sunday was married at St. Peter's Church, in this City, Hyacinth Skerrett, Esq; of Finavarra, in the County of Clare, in the Kingdom of Ireland, to Miss Byrne, only, daughter of the late George Byrne, of Cornell's Court, in the County of Dublin."

Hyacinth is credited with building Finavarra House, the remains of which stand today. Parliamentary papers show he invested in the local fisheries, building a harbour in the Burren in partnership with Henry Persse. He also owned property in Fingias in County Wicklow, through his marriage to Mary Byrne. The records show that he died at Fingias around 1790.

Finavarra House

1. View of Finavarra House from the bay, believed to date from the mid 19th century

2. View of Finavarra House from the front – believed to date from 1890's

The four storeys house, as described by a contemporary in the 1880s, was built on a terrace. It consisted of an underground basement where kitchen staff were housed. On the ground floor was the drawing room, dining room, library, and schoolroom while the 1st and 2nd floors contained the bedrooms. In the 1911 census the house is listed as having thirteen rooms occupied. The same census return showed the outhouses to include two stables, a coach house, cow shed, dairy, piggery, barn, and a turf house Like many houses built in the 18th century, Finavarra House had a tunnel underneath. Although, the entrance is now blocked up, it, according to a local man PJ Linnane, ran from the kitchen to the seashore at the foot of the demesne. There were three entrances to the grounds with two gate lodges. The main entrance consisted of a sweeping avenue of lime trees that ran from the bottom gate house to the house. The same contemporary observer describes the gardens, designed by an Italian landscape artist. The orchard was in a walled garden, well stocked with fruit trees. There was a rose garden with a weeping willow situated behind the house. From the garden a door opened to the roadway and across the road was another door and pathway up through some woods to the top of hill, opening out on a magnificent view of Galway Bay.

The magnificent displays of daffodils described in the 1880's, still bloom today in the demesne, 140 years later. Finavarra House was developed at a time, the end of 18th and early 19th century, when the Irish gentry along with their English counterparts, built estates; large houses with elaborate grounds, including tree lined avenues, large demesnes with sea or river views and walled gardens. Although not as big or as grand as some of the estates of his contemporaries, Hyacinth Skerrett, free of the restrictions that Catholicism would have placed on him, designed his property on a grand scale as becoming to his position in society.

William Major Skerrett

Hyacinth was succeeded by his son, William Major Skerrett (1770 – 1818), who married Mary Jane Roche of Limerick in 1803. Mary Jane bought a substantial dowry to the marriage and under the terms of the marriage settlement, a legal agreement was set up between Mary Jane's father and William Skerrett whereby the Skerrett estate was put in a trust for their heir and descendants for 500 years and could not be broken up or subdivided. Unlike Hyacinth, William remained a Catholic and records for 1810 show he was prominent in fighting for the rights for Catholics in County Clare alongside Daniel O Connell. William and Mary Jane had four daughters and two sons. The Limerick Gazette reported in December 1804, that the wife of William Skerrett gave birth to a son. The understanding is that the child died in infancy Local folklore tells that the family of William Major was cursed. Catching a poor widow filling a bag with dried cow dung from the lawn of his house for firewood, William Major had banished her from his land. Enraged with his pettiness, she wished misfortune on William Major and his heirs, predicting that they would all die young, and never go on to have heirs that would inherit his estate. In Irish Folklore, the widow, being the most vulnerable in society, maintained her power through her curse. William Major, on his death bed with no surviving male heir must have feared that the widow's predictions were about to come through. However, the birth of another son, William after his father's death, ensured an heir for a time at least. William Major and Mary's second son William Joseph, born six months after the death of his father in 1818 became the heir to the estate. According to his great grandson Valentine Williams, William Major had a reputation as a bit of a rake. Valentine's mother had told him of two old bachelors known as Paddy and Johnny Skerritt who helped around the kitchen in her youth but who bore an uncanny family resemblance to the rest of the Sker-rett family.

William Joseph born in 1818, got the name Minor from having inherited the estate while still a 'minor'. Mary Jane, William Major's widow, didn't stay single for long, she re-married in 1819 at Finavarra House not long after the death of her first husband. Her second husband was Peter Blake Morgan, the 3rd son of Charles Morgan, landowner in South Galway. But the marriage was short lived, Mary Jane died two years later in 1821. Peter Blake Morgan continued to live in Finavarra, dying there in 1846.

After the death of their parents, the lands at Finavarra were put under the guardianship of the Court of Chancery and the estate was managed by Peter Blake Morgan on be-half of the children of Mary Jane and William Major. Letters survive from Peter Blake to the authorities, in which he complains that he is facing intimidation from the tenants who were making unreasonable demands on him during the late 1820's when outrages by the Terry Alts were rife in Clare. He petitioned unsuccessfully to be made a local mag-istrate and commissioner of the peace.

The story goes that in 1827 two Comyn brothers from Holliwell were visiting their cousins in Kilcorney when they decided to ride across to Finavarra and bring back two of the Skerrett sisters on the back of their horses to marry them. While the story has romantic connotations, the abduc-tions of eligible 'ladies of fortune' in the early 19th century was not uncommon among the swashbuckling gentry. Once abducted, quite often the women's family had to consent to marriage to the abductor to protect their daughter's honour. In the case of the Skerrett's women, willingly or not, Marga-ret, the eldest Skerrett sister, married Thomas Comyn, heir to the Comyn lands at Holliwell in the Pro Cathedral Dublin in 1827. The second sister Matilda died aged 24, unmarried in Holliwell at the home of her sister in 1830. Her will shows that she died with securities and funds of £2200 in her name which is equivalent to over £200,000 today, indicating that she and her sisters were indeed ladies of fortune. The third sister, Clarinda, married Thomas Comyn's younger brother George in 1835 in the parish church at Oranmore when she was 18. Clarinda had three children with George, before he died in 1839. She subsequently married William D'Alton an attorney and had nine more children.

The fourth Skerrett daughter, Mary Ann married Valentine French. Valentine's brother Anthony was heir to the French family estates in Galway but prevented from inheriting during the Penal Laws because of his Catholic faith. Like many of the native and old Norman Irish gentry, he decided to convert to Protestantism. On his way to swear his renunciation of Catholicism, he was thrown off his horse. Taking this as a sign from God, he decided to remain a Catholic, forfeiting his inheritance and he fled to Italy where he founded a bank called 'French and Lemon.' His brother, Valentine, joined him and following their marriage, Mary Anne Skerrett, and Valentine made their home in Florence.

William Minor attended Trinity College in 1837, before inheriting the estate on reaching the age of 21. Shortly afterwards in 1840 he married Anna McMahon of Firgrove County Clare when she was just 17. The Clare Journal reported on March 2, 1840:

> *"On Wednesday, at the residence of her father, by the Right Rev. Dr. Kennedy, R.C., Bishop of Killaloe, William J. Skerrett, Esq., of Finavarra House, in this county, to Anna, eldest daughter of John McMahon, Esq., of Firgrove. Immediately afterwards they departed for the continent."*

Anna's father had campaigned with Daniel O'Connell during his election in Clare and in the victory procession through Ennis, Anna as a child accompanied the Liberator in his carriage.

William Minor and Anna Skerrett

Anna and William Minor had 14 children, eight of them born before William reached the age of 30. Glimpses of the wealthy and privileged lifestyle they led can be gleaned from frequent mentions in the society columns of the day. They spent the season in Dublin where the Dublin Newspapers reported on their arrival with their entourage, and their attendance in the drawing rooms of Dublin society, the gowns and jewels worn by Mrs. Skerrett and their daughters. In the 1860's they purchased a mansion in Mountjoy Square for which they employed a fulltime cook. A detailed record of his accounts, income, and expenditure from 1857 to 1867, maintained by William Minor, are preserved in the National Library of Ireland. They provide an insight into the lavish lifestyle enjoyed by him and his family.

In 1856 William and Anna took their three older boys to England where they lodged with a tutor for 6 months while William and Anna with Helena, their eldest daughter embarked on a Grand Tour. They travelled first to London before visiting Paris, Dijon, and the South of France. They spent weeks in Switzerland before parting with Helena who stayed there for a further three months as part of her education. With Anna, William returned home travelling through Germany and Brussels. In Brussels he went on a major spending spree. His accounts show his purchases of gemstones, jewellery and, silk dresses for Anna and neckties for himself.

As well as frequent travel trips abroad, his expenditure shows regular purchases of cigars, whiskey and fine wines ordered from Dublin and transported by train to Athenry for delivery to Finavarra. He paid subscriptions to his fellow gentry friends and relations, the Persses of Roxborough and his in-laws, the McMahons of Firgrove for the maintenance of hounds, which allowed him and his sons to take part regularly in local hunts. In 1857 he enrolled his three eldest sons William, John Byrne, and Hyacinth, in Oscott College, a Catholic boarding school near Birmingham. The boys stayed until 1861. His accounts show twice yearly payments to the school for terms April to October and October to March and Christmas boxes delivered to the school in December. Oscott was regarded as one of the most elite Catholic boarding schools in England, attended by the sons of the landed gentry, or at least by those that could afford its fees. The motivation of the Irish gentry in sending their sons abroad was driven by their desire that they should form a network of influential peers and receive an education that would give them professional and social advantage. The younger Skerrett sons, Philip, Charles, Valentine, Frederick, Patrick, and Robert were educated at private boarding schools in Ireland at Tullabeg in Offaly, at St Stanislaus, a Catholic boarding school for younger boys in Tullamore before progressing to senior school at Clongowes. The brothers got mentions in the newspapers for their prominent roles in debating societies and more frequently for their prowess on the sporting field. Summers were spent in Finavarra, where the sons went shooting, hunting, and fishing and played cricket. The Skerrett sons had their own cricket team and their matches against Galway, held in Finavarra became an annual event. One such match reported in the *Galway Vindicator*:

"CRICKET FINAVARA XI v GALWAY XI
The above match was played on Monday on the Finavarra ground, at the Skerrett residence. Owing to the in- clemency of the weather only one innings aside could be played. As will be seen from the

score the home team had an easy win. The visitors were entertained with profuse hospitality at Finavarra House."

In his biography Valentine Williams, (grandson of William Minor and Anna) describes summer trips to Finavarra at the end of the 19th century, swimming at the Flaggy Shore and watching the amazing sunsets over Galway Bay. He describes trips on the Skerrett boat called the Banshee, which was used for sailing from Skerretts' Quay across Galway Bay in all weathers. He describes the remoteness of Finavarra, coming from London where his journey included a three-hour trip by horse and sidecar from Athenry Railway Station to Finavarra. He regarded Finavarra House as primitive in comparison with his home in London; it had no system of plumbing, all water for drinking and washing had to be carried up from the basement and the only lighting consisted of candlelight and lamps. He portrays a place where all his family congregated, and a time when the gentry of Galway, Clare and Limerick took houses in the Flaggy Shore for the summer. A time and place where the upper classes mixed and socialized before the upheavals of the late 19th century bought an end to their privileged existences.

As well as being active in society William Minor was also politically active. He was a Justice of Peace, and he was appointed Sheriff of Clare in 1843. He was involved in the organization of the Famine Relief works in Clare and the Burren and petitioned the English Parliament for relief for the victims. He along with five other candidates sought election as MP for Clare in 1855 although he failed to win the seat. He was appointed Deputy Lieutenant for Clare by Lord Inchiquin.

In Finavarra William Minor was very involved in the running of the estate. Well regarded by his tenants he had a reputation of being a good landlord during the famine era, when many of his counterparts were absentee landlords and ignored the plight of their tenants. While William Minor had ten sons with Anna, eerily, the prophesy of early deaths and heirless sons was one to be fulfilled. It was said, according to Valentine Williams that the swans of nearby Lough Murray, would fly hooting over Finavarra House the night before the death of a Skerrett. Sadly, for the Skerrett family, in the last quarter of the 19th century there were many such occurrences.

Children of William Minor and Anna Skerrett

Alfred, known in the family as Alfie, born in 1846, was the first to die. All that we know about his short life is what can be gleaned from his father's financial accounts. He suffered ill health as a child and William Minor's accounts show he paid Dr Hynes £10 for medicine for Alfie in 1855, two weeks later he paid the priest £2 for Masses for Alfie and on the 24th of December 1855, 6 weeks later, he paid Martin Linnane £5 for a coffin. He purchased black silk dresses for the girls, Alfie's sisters, in mourning for their brother.

Captain William was the eldest, born in 1842 at his mother's family home in Firgrove. Heir to the Skerrett estate his birth was greeted in all the local newspapers. *The Tuam Herald* reported the following:

> *"Great Rejoicing at Finavarra. —On Monday last,' intelligence having reached Finavarra House, the seat of W. J. Skerrett, Esq. that his amiable Lady had given birth an heir to his property. The tenantry, one and all, exhibited their heartfelt pleasure on the joyful occasion. In in the evening bonfires were lighted in the different villages on the estate, and every demonstration of respect and attention was shown to the future representative of the House Finavarra. Mr. Hynes's house at New Quay, presented a brilliant spectacle, being most tastefully illuminated as indeed were in all the houses in the*

neighbourhood. Long may Mr. Skerrett live to enjoy the fond attachment of his tenantry, as exhibited in the present occasion."

After leaving Oscott school near Birmingham, where he had spent his last year as a pupil teacher, William joined the army. His father paid £450 to purchase a commission as an ensign which allowed him to become a lieutenant in the 36th Hereford Regiment in 1865. At the time it was possible to become an army officer by purchasing a commission. This ensured that those who could afford it could become officers. He served in India where he was promoted to Captain. When his father, William Minor, after two years of declining health, died in 1874, Captain William resigned his commission and came back to Finavarra to manage the estate. In June 1876, 18 months after inheriting the estate, he married Helena Reilly of Dublin. Helena, before her marriage, along with her sister is listed as a frequent attendee at the Drawing Rooms in Dublin, where the daughters of the elite were presented at the Lord Lieutenant's Ball. In the Irish Times Friday 31st January 1873 her presence was noted, and her attire described as follows:

"Miss Helena Reilly, 4 Belvedere Place—Train and corsage of the richest white grosgrain trimmed with bouillous of tulle. French blonde, and nouedes of white satin jupon of white poult-de-soie, tastefully trimmed on bretelles with bias folds of satin, soft blush roses, and lily of the-valley. Headdress wreath of white narcissus, court plume and lappets, ornaments pearls."

Helena Skerrett, eldest daughter of William and Anna was also included in the list of those attending the same event. Her clothes are also described in detail including her jewels, diamonds, and emeralds. The wedding of Captain William and Helena Reilly was held in the Pro Cathedral, with 5 priests' celebrants. The groom's address was given as 21 Mountjoy Square, the Skerrett mansion in Dublin. A year later, after a long honeymoon, the couple returned to

Finavarra. News of their homecoming was posted in the Freeman's Journal on Friday 27 July 1877.

> *"Last Wednesday Capt. Skerrett and his young bride were welcomed home to Finavarra, in the north-west of the county Clare, with every mark of affectionate regard, on their return from Dublin. The carriage in which they rode from Oranmore was surrounded at New Quay by an immense gathering of the tenantry and people of the neighbourhood, and they were presented with a hearty address of welcome, which appears in our advertising columns. At the entrance to Finavarra a triumphal arch, forty feet high, decorated with flags and festooned with red and white roses spanned the way, while other floral arches, with waving banners, were raised along the road, The surrounding hills blazed with bonfires, there was an abundant discharge of fireworks, and with flowing hogsheads, merry pipes, and rattling dances the festivities were prolonged long after dark."*

Popular with his peers, locals, and tenants, William was described by his nephew Valentine Williams as a big jovial character with a 48-inch chest. However, a year after his return to Finavarra in June 1878 aged just 36, William died in Finavarra. The cause of death in his obituary stated that while out hunting he had caught a chill and died a few days later. His young bride of 25, Helena was left widowed. She waited for 60 years before she remarried aged 85.

John Byrne, the second son, born in 1844 inherited the estate following the death of his brother William. He had trained to be a doctor and lived in Dublin but after William's death ran the estate and served as Justice of the Peace in Clare. He died of pneumonia three years after William in 1881 aged 37.

Hyacinth, the 3rd son, joined the Royal Navy after leaving boarding school. In 1871, he resigned and trained to become a Catholic priest at Oscott, where he had previously attended school. After his ordination at Oscott he served in a number of parishes in England before returning to serve as a curate in Ballyvaughan, where he was affectionately known as Father Hycie. Following the death of John Byrne, he was next to inherit the estate. When he died in Dublin in 1900, he was the last surviving brother of the Skerrett family.

Philip Huscared, the 4th son, attended St Stanislaus and later Clongowes, making his mark as chairman of the debating society and head boy. He trained in medicine and qualified as doctor, but died in Dublin, aged just 25 in 1875.

Charles, the 5th son attended Trinity College before qualifying as an engineer. One of his duties was to look after the royal train and every time Queen Victoria travelled by train, he went with her to ensure no mechanical failures. He married Ada Mildred, who came from a wealthy Norfolk family. They lived in Thorpe in Norfolk in a house which he named Finavarra House. Following a brain tumour Charles spent the last 3 years of his life in St Georges Lunatic Asylum in Sussex and died there in 1888. Of all the sons he was the only one to have children, a boy and girl, Charles, and Kathleen. Following his death, his wife Ada, abandoning her children, became a nun and entered an enclosed convent in Belgium. Escaping Nazi occupation, she moved to the south of France to a convent near Montpelier where she died in 1942. Her daughter Kathleen was sent to boarding schools and then to Rome to be cared for by an aunt. Kathleen later married the English Counsel General at Milan. Charles, the brother of Kathleen, and only grandson on the Skerrett male line, became a monk in the Abbey of Maredsous in Belgium. When the first school at Glenstal Abbey was opened by monks, transferred from Maredsous, Father Columba Skerrett (as Charles became known) was the first headmaster in 1932. He died in 1936.

Valentine and Robert, the 7th and 8th sons, were twins. Robert emigrated to America but died at sea in a drowning accident. Valentine attended Saint Stanislaus College and Clongowes, like his brothers but returned to Finavarra after leaving school. As his brother Hyacinth had become a priest, Valentine managed the estate in his absence. He served as Justice of Peace and was a member of the Grand Jury for Clare. He is described as a farmer in the Electoral Rolls, renting lands for pasture to local tenants. He involved himself in the relief of poverty and organized concerts at Finavarra House to raise funds for New Quay School. He died in 1895 aged 42 of cirrhosis of the liver and his mother commemorated him with a stained-glass window in New Quay church.

Frederick Thomas the 9th son was born in 1858, He studied at the University of London, after which he trained as a surgeon and joined the British Army. He was stationed from 1885 to 1895 in Burma before transferring to the Cape in South Africa. It was here he met his future bride Edith Rose Kelly whom he married in 1897. She was 17 years younger than him, and they lived for a time in Bury Lancashire. After a short marriage he died in 1899 in Harrogate, the cause of death was Malaria and Acute Intoxication. Edith Rose, the widow of Frederick Skerrett, went back to live with her family following his death. Her second husband was Alistair Crowley, a writer, magician, and occultist, and for a time regarded as the evilest man in Britain. Together they travelled the world and had two children. The first daughter named Nuit Ma Ahathoor Hecate Sappho Jezebel Lilith Crowley, died of malaria and the second daughter, born shortly afterwards suffered from foetal alcohol syndrome. Concerned with his wife's drinking, Alistair divorced her in 1909 and in 1911 he had her admitted to an institution. In 1912 Rose married again, this time Dr Joseph Andrew Gormley. She continued to suffer from alcoholism and dementia and died in 1930.

Patrick de Basterot, the 10th son, like Frederick, he attended the University of London. He too joined the British Army as a doctor and saw service in India, where he met and married an English nurse, Mary Grey. While at home visiting his sister in Eyrecourt in 1896, he fell ill and died of heart failure. He was aged 34 on his death. Mary never remarried. He is also commemorated by a stained-glass window in New Quay church.

William Minor and Anna had 4 daughters. Unlike their brothers, the girls were not expected to pursue careers, instead they were prepared for roles in society which involved marriage to a suitable member of their class.

Helena the eldest married Captain Stephen Cowan in 1864. Captain Cowan had served in the Galway Militia, before returning home to run his family estate at Tullywood Eyrecourt. They had one daughter, Anna in 1866, who never married or had children. Stephen died in 1916, Helena died in May 1917 and her daughter 10 months later in March 1918.

Mary, or *Minnie* as she was called, was born in 1844. Like her sisters, she was presented at the drawing rooms in Dublin, but she clearly decided that the role of wife to a member of the gentry wasn't for her as she became a nun. She entered the Convent of Mercy in Galway in 1873 and was promoted to the role of Reverend Mother before dying in 1923. She was buried in the Magdalen Cemetery in Foster Street Galway.

Matilda, the third daughter and the seventh child was reared by her aunt in Florence. The story told by her son is that Mary Ann Skerrett, who had married Valentine French, finding herself unable to have children, asked Anna and William Minor (her younger brother), while Anna was pregnant with the 7th child, that if the infant was a girl, could she Mary Anne, rear her as her own child. When Matilda was born, she spent the first 4 years in Finavarra, after which, she was whisked off to Florence by Mary Ann and Valentine French, to be reared by them. Growing up, she spent a short time in Boarding School in Dublin before returning to Florence. The family had hoped to arrange for Matilda to marry one of the sons of their gentry friends. Instead, Matilda met George Williams from London who worked as a Reuter's correspondent, and they married in Italy. The children of Matilda and George grew up in London but spent their summers in Ireland at Finavarra and at the home of the French's other relations. Valentine Williams, their 7th child, became a Reuters correspondent, army officer and later a writer of fiction and biography.

Elizabeth was born in 1864, she married Captain Humphry Yonge of the Royal Navy. He had to resign in disgrace following an incident in which his ship caught fire. They had 4 children together. Captain Yonge died in 1902 and Elizabeth in 1912. Their children were looked after by Helena, Elizabeth's eldest sister and Tully Eyrecourt became their new home.

Anna McMahon, wife of William Minor Skerrett outlived all but one of her sons, she died in 1898 in Harcourt Street in Dublin.

The Beginning of The End

After William Minor died in 1874, the estate was in the Court of Chancery as there were several claims on it. The original trust set up by William Major on his marriage to Mary Jane Roche stipulated that the estate and all the income arising from it should pass to the heir. However, in 1810, when the Government ordered the compulsory purchases of land for building the Martello Tower in Finavarra, the monies received by William Skerrett Major were put in stocks and shares. William Minor left this in his will to his eldest children, bar William his heir. The courts allowed this to be distributed. In 1878 on the death of Captain William, Helena, his widow secured occupation of the house, demesne, and gardens, and a guaranteed income of £300 a year from the estate. When her sister was widowed in 1888, Helena invited her and her two sons to come and live in Finavarra House. After the deaths of his older brothers, William and John Byrne, Hyacinth became the heir to the estate.

The Land Wars of 1878-82 was the beginning of the end for Irish landlords. A new confidence was spreading among the tenant farmers, and in the west the era of almost feudal subservience to the landlord was past. Lady Gregory in her biography described her husband's irritation, when driving through his estate at Coole, his tenants no longer doffed their caps on his approach. This era saw tenant farmers throughout the country staging a rebellion against the high rents they were charged. Finavarra was no different. Hyacinth offered the tenants of his estate 25% reduction in rent, a year rent free and 20% reduction in arrears. However, it soon became apparent to the English Government under Gladstone, that the landlord system throughout Ireland was no longer defensible and new legislation was enacted to enable tenant farmers in Clare, like everywhere else, to buy out the land, they and their forebears had farmed for centuries. As part of this legislation most of the Skerrett estate was sold to their tenants. However, the land in the demesne remained the property of the Skerretts. Valentine, and later Frank Sampson, cut down all the trees in the orchard, wood and demesne and sold the timber. Valentine Williams, grandson of William Joseph and Anna, recalls visits back in the early 20th century, describing the neglected lawns and melancholy air that hung over Finavarra House when all the all the surviving Skerretts had died out.

Helena Skerrett

As well as inheriting the use of the house and demesne at Finavarra, Helena, widow of William, by virtue of her marriage settlement and jointure, lay claim to the proceeds of the sale of several properties on the Flaggy Shore, including

Mount Vernon Lodge. She retained the house in Finavarra, often renting it out for the Summer, until the early 20th century. After the death of Hyacinth Skerrett, she mounted a legal challenge to the sale price of the estate to ensure that her income of £300 a year which was part of the terms of her original marriage settlement was secure when the estate was being sold to the tenants through the Land Commission. She later moved to Dublin and lived with her sister first in Pembroke Road before making her home in Monkstown. Together, her and her sister ran a music school in Dublin. She also got frequent mention in the society columns for her attendance at the races and various charity events. In the 1930's she wrote a book "Thoughts and Maxims on Social Life". It was described as follows in a review:

> *"A dainty little volume in suedette binding enclosing a witty, pungent, and varied collection of maxims (other than the threadbare kind) a sort of potted philosophy in the style of the late Lord Dewar. This pretty booklet has been justly described as pleasant companion in whimsical moments."*

A year after Father Columba, the last Finavarra Skerrett in the male line had died, and 60 years since her first marriage, Helena married for the second time in 1937. She was aged eighty-five. Her spouse was George Henry Acton, sixteen years her junior. Under the terms of her first marriage settlement, if Helena had married earlier, it's possible that while there was still a male heir, she would have forfeited her jointure of £300 a year from the Finavarra Skerrett estate and possibly be forced to repay payments previously received. Helena lived for another seven years, dying in Dun Laoghaire, aged ninety-two. Within three months of her death, George Henry Acton had remarried.

The contents of Finavarra House were distributed and the property dismantled in the early 20th century. The front doorway was given to the priest in Kinvara and became the entrance to the parish church. The marble from the fire-places was used in the altar at Ballindereen St Colman's church and the slates used for the roof. Helena's nephew Frank Sampson retained the grounds of Finavarra House and built a bungalow at the back, where he lived until the 1930's. After the death of Hyacinth, the demesne was sold at auction, my grandfather bought the land and later when Frank Sampson (the nephew of Helena Skerrett) left Fina-varra he sold the shell of the house, his bungalow, and gardens to my father.

The Skerretts' vault in Corcomroe Abbey has been sealed up. The following names and dates are inscribed in stone:

William J 1874
William Captain 1878
Philip 1875
Valentine 1895
John B 1881
Anna 1898
Patrick 1896
Alfred 1857

3. Skerretts' family tomb in Corcomroe Abbey

4. Stained glass window memorial to Patrick Skerrett in New Quay church

5. Stained glass window memorial to Valentine Skerrett in New Quay church

6. Photo of Hyacinth Skerrett, divinity student at Oscott 1875 (by kind permission of Birmingham Archdiocesan Archives)

Skerretts Legacy

Today the shell of the main house remains with crumbling masonry, visited by goats. Cattle graze in the demesne on what was once the lawn where cricket was played. The gatehouses are still there. One has been modernized and was sold in recent times by the descendants of the last gatehouse keeper, while the other is in ruins, with its arched lancet windows overgrown with ivy. The walled garden, bereft of trees is still standing, accessed by a gateway decorated with a plaque showing the Skerrett crest and year 1824.

Valentine Williams, grandson of William Skerrett and Anna McMahon published his biography in 1938. In a review in the Irish Independent the correspondent wrote:

"Mr. Williams writes with much pride of his mother's family, the Skerretts of Finavarra, County Clare, where he spent much time in his young days. The last male of the Skerretts died two years ago,

a Benedictine monk in Belgium. Mr. Williams does not appear to complain of democracy in England: but evidently, he does not like it in Ireland because he indulges in a snobbish sneer of lament at the passing of the Irish Government into the hands of "the small shop-keeping class." As the ancestors of whom he boasts so much were the ruling class in his day, and were, on his own statements. mostly drunken wastrels, this country is not likely to suffer too grievously by the change."

It is true that the Skerrett family grew up in a period when being part of the landowning class automatically entitled them to be part of the ruling elite. Four of the brothers served as Justice of Peace, Magistrates, members of the Grand Jury for Clare and Poor Law Board Guardians, taking their place as they each in turn succeeded as heir to the family estate. In the case of Valentine, he filled in for Hyacinth while he served as a Catholic priest. By the mid 1870's it was clear that the lavish spending of the earlier period was no longer sustainable. There could be only one heir; all the other Skerrett sons were required to find careers, which they did in medicine, engineering, and the armed forces. Although Catholic and Irish since Norman times, they evidently saw their loyalty lying with the British ruling authorities and protection of the Empire. This is evidenced by the number of brothers that joined the military services, serving in Burma, India, and South Africa, earning awards and promotions for their service. Their early deaths could be attributed to just bad luck or, some genetic weakness. But for at least four of them, the evidence from the autopsy reports show they were hastened to their graves by excessive drinking.

2. The Tale of the 19th Century Poor in New Quay

Introduction

"They were dying, they were dying,
Where the golden crops were growing,
They were dying, they were dying where crowded herds were lowing,
They were gasping for existence where streams of life were flowing.
And they perish of the plague where the breeze of health was blowing."

The above poem about the famine was composed in Kilfenora and printed anonymously in the Limerick and Clare Examiner 4th January 1851.

The Irish Famine of the 1840s is undoubtedly the darkest chapter in Irish history. The circumstances that allowed the scale of devastation caused by the twin horrors of starvation and disease are almost incomprehensible today. Whilst Ireland was not alone in suffering the effects of the potato crop failure in 1846 and '47, the actions or, in truth, the inaction of the British government and authorities to mitigate the effects led to widespread destitution and emigration. County

Clare along with Galway and Mayo, was among the counties most severely impacted. The number of farm holdings in Clare is said to have dropped by 42% between 1846 and 1851 as a result of deaths, evictions, and emigration.

Writing in a letter to the Munster News in 1851 the parish priest of New Quay, Rev. Coffey, wrote:

"The grimness of the conditions could be inferred by a single fact that the devastation caused by famine and emigration meant that the population of the parish had gone from seven thousand to less than two thousand in the space of three years, a frightful and appalling reduction."

This wasn't the first time that the Rev. Coffey had highlighted the misery and suffering of his flock. In June 1849, he had written to his bishop, Dr Briggs, regarding the dreadful conditions and destitution being experienced in New Quay, conditions which he said made the place a *"mournful celebrity"*. He described:

"Watching the child pine away for want of nourishment, the adult once vigorous, become weak and worn; the parent, for want of any other guardian, bequeathing the care of his children to the relieving officer, the old and infirm wasting away in hunger and thirst; seeing the living dying for want of food, and the dead, buried without coffins." He went on to describe the hopelessness: *"As the scenes of woe multiply and the prospects darkened it suggested to the priest and his people no other options than terror and despair, with the unroofed house, the neglected fields, the overcrowded and enlarged churchyard, all served to convey the desolation, the poverty and the famine deaths that occurred in the district which though once populous and comfortable, will soon become a sheepwalk or a wilderness."*

His message of misery and tale of despair appeared to have hit home, because when the Poor Relief Commission in Dublin selected the most destitute parishes, the Rev.

Coffey was one of ten parish priests in the west and south-west, who were asked to provide more details of the poverty and dire conditions facing their flocks and he received a donation of £10 towards relief.

Pre-Famine Poverty

It has been well documented that the high dependency on potatoes, with a large proportion of the Irish population living at subsistence level, were major factors that led to the high death rates from starvation and disease during the Irish famine. The population of Ireland grew rapidly from the 18th century. The census results show that Clare had a population of 160,000 in 1813, increasing to 209,000 in 1821 and 258,000 in 1831. (Note the 1813 census figures were based on information collected by the local magistrates and may not be as accurate as later census returns). While there are no figures for New Quay for 1813, the total population (for parishes of Abbey and Oughtmama combined) was 2,325 in 1821 and 3,286 in 1831, indicating a rapid rise in population.

In 1834 the British Parliament implemented the Poor Laws in Great Britain. The Poor Laws ensured that the poor were housed in workhouses, clothed and fed. In return for this care, all workhouse residents were expected to work for several hours each day. In 1835 the same Government conducted a survey of the conditions of the poor in Ireland to determine the state of poverty and how it could be alleviated. Abbey and Oughtmama, the current parish of New Quay, were among the parishes selected for the survey. The first-hand accounts of the people of New Quay questioned, gives a good indication of the sorry state of the poor at the time. Among those that provided evidence were 2 farmers, 2 tradespeople (a weaver and a tailor), the local schoolteacher, and the sergeant of the Burrin constabulary. At the time a constabulary barracks was situated in Burrin village, which in the 1830's was centred in Mortyclough.

One of the most telling statements, was from one of the tenant farmers, O Loughlin, who declared. *"That of all the tithes and rents paid, not a penny of it was returned to the parish."* The tithes were paid to the local Protestant church, the nearest church being at Ballyvaughan and in the mid 1830's the main landlords in the New Quay part of the parish were William Minor Skerrett of Finavarra, Burton Bindon of Currenrue (family seat at Clooney) and Bindon Scott of Cahircon, none of whom at the time had their full-time residence in New Quay. With all the monies, rents, tithes, and taxes going outside the parish, the story depicts a community that had to resort to its own resources and got no help from outside.

The answers to the survey questions on the state of vagrancy indicated that the number of beggars in New Quay was on the increase. The situation was at its worst in the months when work was not available, particularly after the harvest and in the summer months when the previous year's potato crop was consumed and before the new crop was available. However, even from the poorest household a beggar would never be turned away, which, when food was scarce, might just be a little straw to sleep on. The sergeant seemed to think this was in part due to a fear of the beggar's curse should he be forced to leave empty handed.

When questioned, about provisions for the old and the sick, those who contributed to the survey, confirmed that there was certainly a shortage of food, clothes, and firewood, and that there was no provision for the aged. These were fully reliant on family or neighbours for help. No public relief had been given in the parish since the famine of 1822. The nearest dispensary for medical help was in Kilfenora, 11 miles away.

The state of widows in New Quay parish, was particularly harsh. Sometimes the community helped by providing labour to till the soil on a Sunday, but often the widow, following the death of her husband, was forced to leave the land as she could not pay the rent. Many survived by living off limpets and mussels from the seashore, but it came with the risk of catching dysentery or cholera from contaminated shellfish. In previous times, many widows had made a living by spinning flax to be sold to buyers from the north, but this type of work had dried up. (From the late 1820's machines had been introduced in Ulster, that enabled linen to be spun faster and cheaper than by hand.) John Hynes, one of the contributors to the survey, employed some widows for spinning wool but as the price of wool was so low, it gave a very poor return.

But it wasn't just the beggars, the widows, the old or the infirm who lived a precarious existence. A large proportion of the population survived as labourers, these in most instances, known as cottiers, were effectively landless. Unlike the tenant farmers who leased land on an annual term, the cottiers rented conacre which meant they had the use of the land, sometimes just a few acres or less, to grow potatoes, for a season. They lived at subsistence level, depending on potatoes to provide food for their families as they had no money.

John Hynes, a farmer surveyed, told that he had in previous years had to look to Connemara to get labourers and pay their fare across Galway Bay, but now there was a surplus of labourers in New Quay. Quite often no money changed hands, their rent for conacre was paid in labour. The labourer worked for the farmers or landlord for so many days per acre of conacre. There was pride in having a holding, whether a piece of ground for potato growing, conacre or renting grazing land. For those who worked for money, the average wage for an agricultural labourer in New Quay, according to those interviewed, was 6d a day for a short day or 9d for a long day and most were employed for just half the year in spring and at harvest.

Some of the local tenant farmers, who had small holdings, the surveyors were told, supplemented their income as agricultural labourers. While the average size of farm in the parish was 20 acres, a minimum of 10 acres was required to feed a family. It was common practise for the head of a family to give a portion of his land to each son as they married. The last to get married usually got the father's cabin and his portion of land. The father was then dependent on the family to provide for him. Quite often they could not afford to. The father would often try to grow potatoes among the rocks and marginal land so as not to be a burden to their family. Similar to what was happening all over the west of Ireland, the practise of division and subdivisions led to diminishing size of holdings, and all ended up poorer. The local clergy had tried to discourage people from marrying so young by increasing the cost of the ceremony, but the reality was the people just borrowed more to get married so they could have some independence. The population was increasing, and the majority had no other means of subsistence other than living off the land. In the competition for land many offered increased rents higher than they could afford, but this meant they got dispossessed when falling into arrears. It was impossible for a labourer to put money aside for family in case of his death. No assistance was provided by the landlords in New Quay. Although not common, in cases of extreme distress in the past there had been collections by the Catholic clergy to support those in dire circumstances.

Following the report of the Royal Commission on the Poorer Classes in Ireland between 1833 and 1835, the government implemented the Irish Poor Law Act of 1838. Three poor law commissioners divided Ireland into poor law unions, in which paupers would receive poor relief (either workhouse or outdoor relief) paid for by a poor rate. The Irish Board of Works was also set up in the 1830's and among its responsibilities was building a number of new roads, particularly in the remoter regions of Ireland. As well as improving communication the development of new roads also gave employment to the poor in areas where work was scarce. The road between the New Line and the Martello Tower in Finavarra was built in 1841. In 1846, William Minor Skerrett gave Rev Jackson, the curate for New Quay, a half-acre site for a Protestant church at the Flaggy Shore. Two years later the Burren Roads Committee agreed to use available funds to build a road to the church, extending the road along the Flaggy Shore. However, the problems of widespread poverty and destitution did not go away, and the population continued to increase.

By 1841, according to the census returns, the combined population of Abbey and Oughtmama parishes was 3,517. Recognising that the primary source of the misery and wretched state of the vast population could be traced to the system under which land was occupied and owned, the British Tory Government under Robert Peel set up another commission in 1843 to investigate the state of land tenancies in Ireland. This was called the Devon Commission. It was named after William Cortney, the 10th Earl of Devon who headed up the commission. The findings in 1845 reported that the population of Ireland had increased to close on 8 million people and concluded that the leases, while favourable to the landowners, were unfair to the tenants. Most Irish tenants had no form of protection; they could be evicted on the whim of the landlord. They also had no claim on what was called the Ulster Custom of landholding - this would have granted tenants the "3F's": Free sale, fixity of tenure, and fair rent. The Devon Commission was too late to prevent the famine, but it did galvanize change that came afterwards.

As part of the investigation, the commission interviewed numerous parties to collect evidence of the situation in land holdings and relationships between landlord, tenant and the landless. Burton Bindon, oyster magnate and landlord for Munnia, Currenrue and Rossalia, was one of the people that gave evidence in Gort, and his testimony provides a valuable source as to the state of the tenants and landless on his estates, particularly in the Burren. His evidence showed that the conditions in New Quay had not improved since the 1835 survey and for a lot of the cottier class had got worse. The development of a new quay in the 1820's and the prospering of the oyster trade in 1820s and 30s offered opportunities for employment for those who had no access to a farm tenancy, but it was a two-edged sword. While it drew many to New Quay, competition for work was fierce, it meant that wages remained low and rents for conacre remained high.

According to Bindon's evidence his estates, covering both Clooney and the Burren, constituted 1300 acres of land. This included 400 acres that he had cleared in his words from what was previously 'a perfect sheet of rock and stones at a cost of 2 pounds an acre'. He told that in one field alone he had employed 65 girls for a month at a rate of 4d a day to pick the stones to clear the field. His evidence states that he employed on average 300 – 350 people a day, 200 men and 100 to 150 women. If he needed them, he declared he could call on the services of 1000 men, such was the level of poverty and desperation for work where whole families relied for subsistence on the measly wage he offered. He had paid men 8d a day, but this had been reduced to 7d and women got paid 4d a day. Many of the workforce came long distances daily to get the work and if he could guarantee year-round work, the men would do it for 6d a day. Separately he employed many women, to work on his oyster beds, these he paid 3d a day or 1d an hour from 11 to 2 each day from September to May. The people he employed, scraped by, living in makeshift cabins, many renting a few acres of what he called mock land. This was marginal grass land that was burned and then cultivated for potatoes. He described it as follows:

"Those who have no land, rent a small patch for the cultivation of potatoes. This is generally called 'mock' by the people of the West, and in other parts of Ireland it is termed 'conacre.' In the district of which I am now speaking the average rent charged for 'conacre' is £4 an acre, but in other places along the coast it rises so high as £6, £8, and even £10 an acre for bog land which the tenant must manure at great labour and expense. Persons living near the sea can easily obtain seaweed, sand, and shells for manure, and this fact will account for the comparative density of the population along the coast. Farms which border on the sea are much coveted, because of the privilege given to the tenant of collecting seaweed to manure his own land, he gathers as much more as he can, and carries it to Ennis or some other inland place, where he finds a ready sale for all he brings to market, and thus obtains a few pounds, which enable him to pay his rent or to procure food for his family."

A visitor to the Burren in the 1840's wrote that he counted over forty horses with panniers lined up on the sea road by the shore at Munnia, waiting to take harvested seaweed inland for sale. Bindon owned the seashore bordering his land, and the seaweed, when sold as a fertiliser was a lucrative business.

The men observed with the horses would largely have been employed by Bindon. Bindon explained to the Devon Commission that the landlords claimed title to the seaweed harvested between the high and low tide mark while the seaweed beyond the low tide could be harvested by anyone. It was quite common for three or four men to band together and buy a boat for £3 or £4 to collect seaweed. They had invented a pole with a cross bar to twist and pull the seaweed from the sea beyond the low tide marks. A boat load of it could fetch 6s. There were often disputes and fights for the seaweed between the locals and the boatmen from the Claddagh in Galway, whose boats circled Galway Bay. Bindon paid for seaweed to be harvested and gathered from the shore and transported inland, often up to 25 miles, for sale to farmers. Sea wrack was a particular type of seaweed that was thrown up after a storm. There was often enough of this to manure up to 600 acres and it could be sold at 3s a load. He adopted a system of planting rocks and stones on the coast to encourage growth and increase the amount of seaweed. While the labour cost of moving the rocks to the seashore amounted to £2 an acre, this could make the seashore worth between £6 to £10 an acre in seaweed production. The importance of seaweed was enshrined in the ancient Irish Laws of Property. In Gaelic Ireland reaching back to the 6th century, the value of access to a "productive rock" (i.e., with seaweed and shellfish) added the equivalent of 3 cows to the value of a holding. However, anything brought in from the sea (beyond nine waves from the shore) was the property of the finder.

Bindon said it was quite common for the poor people to grow wheat and plough the ground again to grow potatoes in the same year. While seaweed was not as good as animal manure, it certainly gave the people living near the coast the advantage of a more fertile crop and many would have starved without it. Bindon's last comments to the commission were that the wretched state and misery of the poor and population growth could not continue and could only end in disaster. This 'disaster' occurred within two years of his giving evidence.

Famine

Blight in potatoes was first observed along the east coast of Ireland in September '45. Throughout the autumn and winter, it became clear that the whole country was impacted, and disaster loomed for a population which had a high dependency on potatoes for their subsistence. Robert Peel, the British Tory Prime Minister, made aware of the scale of the problem, acted quickly to put relief measures in place. A central Relief Commission was set up to coordinate the relief from Dublin with local commissions put in place in each Poor Law District to manage the local effort to alleviate the distress, including public works to provide employment. To prevent food price inflation, Peel purchased £100,000 worth of Indian Meal in the US to be imported to Ireland, for sale to the poor or free distribution to the truly destitute.

The earliest evidence of the potato famine in New Quay are letters from William Minor Skerrett to the Relief Commission requesting help. Skerrett was spending the season in Dublin and Lucius O'Brien MP for Clare was on a grand tour of Europe when news of the famine spread. Skerrett was told that over 350 people had gathered in New Quay demanding work so they could provide food for their starving families. Concerned that the threats of starvation could lead to violence, he returned immediately to Finavarra. From there he wrote to the Relief Commission, requesting immediate assistance, explaining people were starving as a result of the potato failure and with no means to purchase food, labour mut be provided through public works. In his letter, he stated that he would be setting up meetings with the cess payers i.e., the local rate payers, to agree schemes for employment. The response he received to his letter, agreed that engineers and surveyors would be directed to organise public work where there was money available to pay for them.

Another letter was received from the Dublin Relief Committee in November requesting that a depot be set up in Ballyvaughan for the import and distribution of the Indian Meal, purchased by Peel. A collection among local property owners and clergy raised £21. This amount, plus a generous donation of £30 from the Calcutta Fund in India was to be used to alleviate the distress. One of the first places to send money to Ireland in 1846 was Calcutta. Donations came from across all sectors of society, but particularly from the British Army serving there. Many of the soldiers were Irish born. Three of William Skerrett's own sons were to serve in India. A decision was made to set up a separate Abbey and Oughtmama Relief committee. William Skerrett was chairman, Father O'Fay (the Catholic parish priest) treasurer and Rev. Fulham (the Protestant minister for New Quay) was the clerk. Lucius O'Brien, the MP for Clare was overseer of the relief for county Clare. It was agreed with him that the grain received in Ballyvaughan would be distributed between local parishes in proportion to the population. The coast guards in Ballyvaughan were responsible for the distribution. Father O'Fay had requested 400 tickets, from the Central Relief Commission i.e., approval to employ 400 men on the public works. The Green Road, which runs along the north side of Abbey Hill from Corker Hill to the church in Beagh, was built as part of the relief works. The ruins of the grain store built for distribution still stand today on the Green Road.

When the second potato failure came in 1846, Peel's Tory government had been replaced by the Whigs under John Russell. The Irish famine and the urgent need for new food supplies led Robert Peel to force through the repeal of the Corn Laws, despite opposition from his own party who were generally the supporters of the landed interest, but it also led to his downfall. The prevailing economic views of the new Whig administration were laissez faire, i.e., nonintervention, and to let market forces resolve the problems. Complicated procedures for the central administration of public works through the Board of Works in Dublin, were put in place, which caused delays in bringing relief to those in need. During a harsh winter, there was no food left and the famished people were desperate. Conditions continued to deteriorate as fever, typhus and dysentery contributed to the high mortality rates. Reliance on charity is evidenced from the newspapers in Jun 1848; the *Tipperary Vindicator* wrote: *"The Rev. Messrs. Jackson and Coffey, acknowledge from the Society Friends ten barrels of Indian meal for the poor of New Quay."*

7. The Green Road built as part of the Famine Public Works relief schemes in 1847.

By June '47 the Whig government, had had enough. The problems with the Irish poor were not going away. They blamed the Irish landlords, for the state of the country. They, the landlords, were seen as the architects of the conditions causing these problems and the Government decided that any further relief required should be borne by the local ratepayers and passed a Poor Law Extension Bill. There were two clauses in the bill which were to be particularly harsh and were to have dire consequences, leading to radical changes in the occupation of small holdings. The first was the quarter acre clause proposed by William Gregory.

The name Gregory has survived in the Irish history books largely from the fame of Lady Augusta, (founder of the Abbey Theatre). As a 60-year-old widower, William Gregory married her when she was 28. But Gregory was also an influential politician, serving as an MP first for Dublin and later Galway. With his family seat in Kiltartan, he retained a local reputation as a just and fair landlord during the famine years. The infamous "quarter acre", or Gregory clause as it became known, meant that any family holding more than a quarter of an acre could not be granted relief, either in or outside the workhouse, unless they abandoned their tenancy. The impact of the clause was severe, and the name Gregory became widely detested. No one wanted to give up their tenancy rights as it meant that they would be homeless when they left the workhouse. The refusal of many to give up their tenancies, meant thousands more died needlessly for want of relief. It was said that Gregory, never regretted it and until his dying day was convinced that the clause saved Ireland from an ever-ending cycle of pauperism.

The distress in New Quay caused by famine and disease got frequent mention in the press. Rev. Coffey had replaced Father O'Fay as parish priest of New Quay in 1847 and frequently called attention to the distressed state of his parishioners. In 1847 the Repeal Association had written to the Irish Catholic priests asking them to account for the impact of the famine in their parishes. Known as the Death Census, this was initiated for the purpose of raising awareness to the outside world the extent of the misery caused by the depth and scale of the famine. While there are no surviving returns for New Quay (Rev Coffey declared in one of his letters that the dead were too numerous to count) there are returns for Kinvara Union and for Ennistymon and Kilfenora. Father Francis Arthur of Kinvara claimed of the 10,000 people in the union which covered parishes of Kinvara, Durras and Killeen, there were only 400 people who weren't in need of relief. In the period October 1846 to March 1847 148 people in his union had died of starvation and from dysentery caused by eating bad foods such as nettles and seaweed. The people in ordinary times had depended for subsistence on the potato and selling of seaweed. But with failure of potato the demand for seaweed as a fertiliser had fallen. The parish priest of Ennistymon John Sheehan counted 352 dead in the workhouse in the period, October 1846 to March 1847. The Ennistymon Workhouse served the Ennistymon Union which in this period included the parish of New Quay. According to Rev Sheehan, whole families had been wiped out by lack of food and disease. People only came to the workhouse as a last resort when every other resource open to them had been exhausted. They were bought, emaciated starving creatures, on carts, like wounded men on a battlefield, bringing with them famine fever, dysentery, and disease to the workhouse.

In 1849 the *Limerick and Clare Examiner* printed the following:

> *"The state of the poor in New Quay is not to be described. They are dying and pining away in hopeless want and misery. Certainly, they get outdoor relief and there can be no fault ascribed to the relieving officer in the performance of his duties. But still the havoc proceeds. The clergymen Rev. Mr Coffey is also in great distress and nearly as poor as his distressed parishioners."*

On the 10th of January 1849, the *Limerick and Clare Examiner* reported on the trial of 12 "*desperate creatures*" from New Quay who, driven by starvation and not having received their meal rations had attacked the car bringing the meal to the depot:

> *"About a dozen poor wretched creatures from the New Quay area were, yesterday, found guilty at the Ennis Sessions for attacking a car laden with meal for the depot at New Quay. They took about a stone, which they divided among each other. They said they were*

refused their rations. They were sentenced to 5 weeks from the date of their committal which expires tomorrow, in order, the Barrister remarked they should get their dinner tonight, and breakfast tomorrow, before entering the long journey home of 24 miles."

A term in gaol gave them temporary relief from the hunger that faced them outside. In February 1849, the same newspaper noted that 100s of people were still starving in New Quay and the clergy in misery. The reporter wrote that the lives of several famished creatures were dependent on the benevolence of the only resident proprietor, Mr Skerrett.

Another clause of the infamous Poor Law Extension Bill required landlords to pay tax for each holding on their estate, including those valued at £4 and below. Landowners, who already had lost a large part of their rents because of the famine, now faced another blow to their income. This was to be particularly severe in the west and disadvantaged areas where there were such a huge proportion of small holdings for which the landowner was liable to pay a tax per holding. This gave rise to mass clearances and evictions. In New Quay today few horror stories have been passed down of mass evictions by landlords, yet the population statistics show that whole villages disappeared in the famine years '46 to '51. In 1851 the following was published in the Munster News on Wednesday 08 October:

"It is the Arabia Petra of this otherwise fertile and beautiful Island; and the solemnity of its aspect is even enhanced by ruins of dwellings once occupied near small patches of earth, amid the wilderness of crags. At Burren and New Quay, everywhere in fact, vestiges of eviction were painfully perceptible. In Chapels the congregations were "thinned" down to one half; and further on to Kinvara, eviction had done the last practicable deed of unsparing depopulation."

As the population diminished through disease, famine and emigration, many landlords plunged deeper into debt. The nature of Irish property law meant that creditors could not force the sale of the landlords' assets and the legal principle of entail prevented the property from being transferred until all debts and encumbrances had first been paid. For years, even before the famine, Irish landlords had been living beyond their means. Taking their cue from their English counterparts they lived extravagantly, travelling extensively, supporting their Dublin town houses and country estates but without the income to support their lifestyle. The Whig government had little patience for the Irish landlords who were mainly Tory and in 1848 and '49 passed the Encumbered Estate Acts. Estates could be compulsorily sold on the petition of a creditor or the landlord himself.

In 1854 John Scott's estates in New Quay, including the townlands of Mortyclough and Ballyvelaghan, were sold through the Encumbered Estates Court. The Skerrett family, though heavily in debt, retained their lands around Finavarra and New Quay until the 1890's when the Land Acts supported tenant farmers' land purchases. Burton Bindon auctioned all his possessions and left for Australia in 1849. Returning in 1852, his lands in the Burren and Clooney were sold through the Encumbered Estates Courts. The Dublin Evening Mail reported on Thursday 19 January 1865:

> *"The Burren Estate. —The two remaining unsold lots of the Burren estates have been purchased by private sale by William Lane Joynt, Esq., agent to Lord Anally, for £11,000. Thus, the noble lord has become the owner all the Burren estate of Mr. John L. Kernan. The noble lord is also the owner of the Duke of Buckingham's estate at Ballyvaughan; Mr. Burton Bindon's, at Currenrue, on which are the famous oyster beds; Mr. John B. Scott's, at New Quay; Sir Hugh Dillon Massey's Broadford estate, and Mr. John Westropp's, at Kilkeryne. These represent one of the largest territorial possessions in the hands any peer or commoner in Clare."*

Captain Henry White and later his son Luke White MP (who also held the title Lord Anally), were owners of vast estates with their family seat at Luttrelstown Castle in Dublin. William Lane Joynt, who served as Mayor of Limerick and Mayor of Dublin, was the agent for Lord Anally in the Burren with a home at Clareville, Ballyvaughan. In 1895, while loading a revolver, he blew his finger off and he died shortly afterwards of complications following an operation on his hand. Lord Anally continued to own most of the land in New Quay, Carran and Ballyvaughan up until the land was purchased by the tenants following the Land Acts of the late 19th century.

The Workhouses

In 1838 under the new Ireland Poor Laws, the country was divided into 150 unions and 2049 electoral divisions based on estimates of the population. Ennistymon was the union centre for North Clare and a workhouse was built there for the destitute. When the famine struck, it became clear that the impact of the famine was not evenly dispersed and the unions and workhouses in some areas of the country particularly in the west and southwest were not able to cope with the numbers of poor and destitute requiring help. Ennistymon Union was one of those highlighted as requiring external relief, marked as an area with one of the highest rates of poverty and having one of the least resources to pay. Auxiliary workhouses in Ennistymon Union were opened in Ballyvaughan, as well as Lahinch, Rathkeale, Sandfield and Milton Malbay, all to accommodate those requiring help. In 1848 it was agreed that the Union of Ennistymon should be split in three, Ennistymon, Corofin and Ballyvaughan (which included the parish of New Quay). Under the Poor Law Amendment legislation in 1847 it was required that the rate payers contribute in proportion to the indoor relief in the workhouse for the paupers from their area. The local landlords were now elected to the Ballyvaughan Board of

Guardians, but they were also the ratepayers, so it was in their interest to keep costs down. The auxiliary workhouse in Ballyvaughan was unable to accommodate the numbers requiring help and many ended up in Ennistymon and Milton Malbay, and Lahinch. As the cost for those was borne by the Ballyvaughan Union ratepayers, the Ballyvaughan Board of Guardians were distrustful of the charges imposed by Ennistymon, believing that many of those charged for were already dead or had left the workhouse. In order to check the number of inmates from the Ballyvaughan district they frequently instructed the Ennistymon workhouse officers to assemble the workhouse inmates from their area for inspection.

The local inspector reported a distressing incident in October 1850, whereby the staff for the auxiliary workhouse in Milton Malbay, were ordered to send 100 boys (paupers and orphans native to the district covered by the Ballyvaughan Union with an average age of 9), from Milton Malbay Workhouse to Ennistymon to be inspected. The boys were given weak gruel at 7 a.m. before walking to Ennistymon, arriving at 2 o' clock for the inspection. They were released at 5 o'clock to walk the return journey on a wet and stormy night having been given no food or drink since breakfast. Those that made it back were exhausted and famished. The matron described having to prise open the frozen jaws of some of the younger children so they could be fed hot milk. Some didn't make it back, lying by the roadside unable to carry on while one poor child was found blown into a ditch and dead from hunger and exhaustion. The Poor Law Inspector demanded a murder enquiry and opened an inquest to determine who was to blame. The Ennistymon Workhouse staff said they had not received any instructions from the Ballyvaughan Board of Guardians to feed the children, but the Ballyvaughan Guardians claimed it wasn't their responsibility.

In 1855, the auxiliary workhouse in Ballyvaughan was replaced with a new building, that could house 500 inmates. Jobs for staff to run the workhouse were advertised in the local papers. The job of Master of the Workhouse was advertised at £20 and Matron at £12 a year as well as positions for School Master at £5 and School Mistress at £4. For many, going to the workhouse was their only option when they had lost everything else. The paupers were treated like prisoners and subjugated to the iron rule of the master; they had to give up their own clothes and as a deterrent, the conditions were designed so that they had poorer clothes, poorer diet, and poorer lodging than the labourers outside. While for some it was a last attempt at survival, for many it hastened their early deaths from diseases which were rife in the workhouse. The records for the Ballyvaughan Workhouse have not survived, so we cannot tell how many of the inmates were from New Quay. However, each year the Returning Officer published the rates chargeable to each electoral division within the Ballyvaughan Union, which included Abbey and Oughtmama. The rate books for most years from 1852 show that charges were evenly distributed across each parish suggesting that the poor in the workhouses came in equal measure from New Quay, Carron, Ballyvaughan and other parishes. In the years after the famine, from 1852 and 1863 the numbers in the workhouse were falling steadily as conditions improved and those that could emigrated. Notes from the Ballyvaughan Board of Guardians published in the Clare and Ennis Journal in August 1864, show that there was a temporary blip in that year as the numbers jumped. The paper describes the outrage of the members of the board as they noted the sudden influx of unmarried mothers and illegitimate children from New Quay to the workhouse.

"REPORT OF THE COMMITTER ON THE STATS OF THE WORKHOUSE

In the year 1860 the total number of inmates in the workhouse amounted to only 83. In July 1864, (this year) the numbers had increased to 216 of that number 60 were composed of illegitimate children and their mothers. The total number now in the house is 185. Of that number there were in the house on Saturday last, 32 illegitimate children and 18 of their mothers, making a total of 50 of that class. Of that number of 50 from all the union, 32, including 19 children belonging to the electoral division of Abbey, (Newquay); but in July last the number of that disreputable class, from Abbey, amounted to 42. However, since the Chairman's denunciation of the profligacy of that parish, 10 of that 42 have been taken out of the workhouse. The number of other cases—such as infirm old persons, and fever cases from Abbey, now amounts to only 11 persons. The estimated rate for the half year on Abbey, will 2s in the pound, amounting to 4s for the year, should the immoral women from Abbey be harboured with their children in the workhouse, and which confiscating rates will tend to embarrass the property industry of that electoral division, except where there are such wealthy proprietors as Lord Annally, and Messrs. Skerrett and French. The Committee have investigated each case in the union, and they are of the opinion that action cannot be sustained in the quarter sessions court against the putative fathers of any of the illegitimate children the workhouse. At the end of the meeting the chairman asked for a full investigation into 'the excess of immorality which exists in one of the Unions of our county."

At the September meeting members were told that following the investigation, at least one woman claimed a member of the board of Guardians was the father of her illegitimate children. Although not wanting to believe her, the members did much pontificating on the evils of illegitimacy being allowed to proliferate and implemented more stringent criteria for any new unmarred women with their children entering the workhouse.

In 1896 a parliamentary report showed that conditions in Ballyvaughan workhouse were a *"litany of wretchedness, misery and squalor*". A visit by a commission from the British Medical Team had found the male inmates using a mortuary as a day room and lounging and smoking on the shelves intended for the dead bodies. While the report recommended the workhouse should be shut down, it remained in existence until it was demolished in 1923. The census results for 1891, 1901 and 1911 show that about 100 residents were still in the workhouse throughout this period. On the census returns most of the residents were categorised as insane, infirm, elderly or orphans and for the infirm the workhouse also served as a hospital.

Post Famine

Reports in the papers from 1850 and 1851 showed that the conditions for the poor in County Clare did not improve in the years immediately following the famine. In 1851, Rev Coffey was called to attend to a dying child in Aughinish. He described entering a hovel close by the shoreline, where he found what he thought was a seven-year-old child and his shock and horror when told that it was an emaciated starving 20-year-old women. His story was one of many which highlights that the distress of his parishioners was still continuing and had not gone away, although the famine was officially over.

Letters from Pierce Creagh, (Charman of the Board of Guardians of the Ballyvaughan Union) to Lord Russell, (First Lord of her Majesty's Treasury) from 1851, survive which also tell of the ongoing distressed state of the district covered by the Ballyvaughan Union. He complained that the rate payers were unable to pay the poor rate required for the relief of the destitute of the district. It's clear from reports in the paper and from Creagh's letters that the devastation from the famine around Ballyvaughan continued. Creagh stated that because of large scale emigration of farmers and able-bodied men, the Ballyvaughan Union was left with a disproportionate number of paupers, particularly women and children which were putting an increasing and unjust load on the ratepayers. Creagh requested that the government provide money from the Rate in Aid fund, a central fund which had been set up to advance loans to distressed unions for the relief of poverty. He was also seeking a revaluation for tax purposes, taxes and rates for the district were based on a pre famine valuation of the land which was no longer realistic. According to Creagh, large areas of the land were now laid waste, the number of sheep was one third and the number of cattle a quarter of what it was before the famine. The drop in prices of agricultural produce and disastrous influence of the famine meant that Ballyvaughan Union now suffered more than any other district in Clare.

In another letter of 1851, he stated that the population for the district of the union, had been reduced to 50% of what it was prior to the famine and that 75% of the population was dependent on indoor or outdoor relief and as there were no opportunities for trade, manufacturing, or commerce it was impossible for a quarter of the population to support three quarters in idleness. The rate payers would be forced to sell all their stock if the rates requested of them were to be paid. Although the numbers requiring aid were widespread, according to Creagh, William Skerrett had been able to give extensive employment in his demesne to the poor from his estate which had served to reduce the numbers otherwise dependent on aid. The employment Creagh referred to include the construction of the Protestant church and lodges William Skerrett built along the Flaggy Shore.

Creagh, in his letters, also referred to assisted emigration. It was found to be cheaper to pay for an individual or family to emigrate to Australia, Canada or America than maintain them in the workhouse. The Union had originally obtained funding to sponsor 2 girls from the Ballyvaughan district for emigration to Australia. This had in 1851 extended to 100 and 100 to America. However, no evidence has come to light to confirm the number of girls, if any, that emigrated under this scheme.

Population Changes

If the numbers, given by Rev. Coffey of the changes in population in New Quay following the famine are correct, New Quay lost over two thirds of its population in the famine years. How many died of starvation, disease, moved to the workhouse, or fever hospital in Kinvara, or how many emigrated we cannot tell as figures providing such breakdown do not exist. The Valuation maps of the 1840's show closely packed settlements or villages in marginal areas such as along by the sea between Cartron and the quay at New Quay. The census summaries provide a good illustration of the changing circumstances in New Quay, parish of Abbey and Oughtmama between 1821 and 1881.

	1821	1831	1841	1851	1861	1871	1881
Abbey Parish							
Abbey East			19	13	4	7	5
Abbey West			140	85	103	92	65
Ailwee			7	3	7	4	3
Ballyhehan			104	68	39	46	38
Ballyvelaghan			263	291	346	239	240
Cartron			17	4	8	9	10
Currenrue			133	81	61	42	35
Dooneen			152	107	97	80	96
Moneen			19	8	6	5	5
Mortyclough			126	83	69	42	57
Munnia			336	93	70	49	50

Rossalia			64	13	34	39	24
Sheshia			62	53	43	31	31
Creg Town				100			
Abbey Total	**1882**	**2025**	**1442**	**1002**	**887**	**715**	**643**
Oughtmama Parish							
Aughawinnan			94	60	37	35	49
Aughinish			30	31	164	151	132
Beagh			76	37	25	31	21
Cragbally-conell			9	15	6	11	7
Deelin Beg			109	7	10	17	5
Deelin Mor			21	11	9	7	11
Finavara Demesne			26	22	21	5	5
Gortboyheen			33	6	4	15	16
Gortaclare			92	49	77	51	46
Kilweelran			98	30	27	19	42
Knockycallan			33	15	10	14	16
New Quay			178	43	92	79	77
Oughtmama			123	92	57	78	68
poulaphuca			13	7	9	9	10
Rine			16	48	277	187	143
Slievecarran			17	11	12	6	4
Turlough			400	263	203	136	122
Aughinish Town			312	201			
Finavarra Town			303	245			
Total Oughtmama	**443**	**793**	**2075**	**1133**	**1040**	**871**	**796**
Grand Total Abbey & Oughtmama	**2325**	**2818**	**3517**	**2135**	**1927**	**1586**	**1439**

Table 1. 19th century Census Summaries by Parish/Townland

Notes

The 1821 and 1831 census reports were not always accurate, and the boundaries between Abbey and Oughtmama changed for 1841. So, when Abbey and Oughtmama are taken together the numbers show a steady increase in population from 1821 to 1841 and a continuous drop post famine from 1851. From 1861, Finavarra Town is included with Rine and Aughinish Town included with Aughinish, and Creg town included with Ballyvelaghan. A settlement that had over 20 houses huddled together was categorised as a 'town'. In 1821 Burrin town and Beagh town were shown separately and for 1841 and 1851 both Aughinish and Finavarra were reported as towns.

After the famine, houses and farm homesteads became more dispersed. The practise of sub dividing the land by giving each member of a family a portion of land, which had been the practice since early Gaelic times and enshrined in Irish Brehon Laws, stopped. The farm or tenancy was now passed on to one member or abandoned as siblings emigrated or remained unmarried.

The claims of Rev. Coffey that the population was over 7000 at the time famine struck, if accurate would suggest that it doubled between 1841 and 1847, which is possible but if true would be the result most likely of new people coming into the parish, availing of opportunities for employment rather than the natural birth rate increase. One of the townlands in Abbey most impacted by the famine numbers was Munnia. In 1841 the population was 336 which went down to 93 in 1851 and continued to decline. The population that disappeared was drawn from the landless class that Bindon had spoken about, those that relied on conacre and the miserable wages from his employment, in the nearby oyster banks and seaweed industries, a livelihood which was only sustainable when the families had a potato crop to feed themselves. Captain Wynne, who was Inspector of Public Works for Clare Relief of Distress in the County of Clare reported that in the parish of Clondagad alone the population had increased by a third, between 1841 and 1846, the eve of the famine. He put the increase down to incomers from the southern counties, drawn by the opportunities for seaweed trading. The population explosion, he explained, meant that the coastal districts all along the west coast of Clare was one giant conacre farm. where families lived at subsistence level on the pennies, they could earn from seaweed harvesting.

As a result of the Poor Law amendments in 1848, landlords everywhere sought to rid their land of small holdings, for which they would be liable for rates. The clearances and evictions of 1000's of families from the Vandeleur estates in the Union of Kilrush were infamous, but little is documented of evictions from lands in Abbey and Oughtmama. It was commonly known until recently that a pre famine village, known as Shawnwalla, existed at the back of the hill beside Cartron. During the famine years the families abandoned the hillside, and many moved to Cregg. The mountain top near Shawnwalla is littered with oysters and cockle shells. This is a legacy of the diet of the poor people who lived there but also derived from those shells entangled in seaweed used as fertiliser by the people who dragged it from the shore to fertilise the land between the rocks.

Cregg town is first recorded in the Census of 1851. When Burton Bindon put his estates up for sale in 1853, he wrote that there was a spit of land in Munnia for which Lord Inchiquin had stipulated, when he sold the Munnia and Rossalia estates to Frances Bindon 100 years earlier, that no rent or taxes would ever be chargeable. So, this spit of land became Cregg town, where the poor evicted from Munnia, and other townlands-built cabins rent free by the lake. 22 houses were recorded in Cregg in 1851 with a population of 100 people. The population was seventy women and thirty men. Those that could leave had left, leaving widows and daughters behind. In 1861 Cregg was included in Ballyvelaghan, but it is one of the few places where numbers increased from 1851 and 1861, indicating people were still being evicted and making their homes at Cregg, where cabins could be built rent and rate free. The houses were crammed in along a road known as Patrick Street.

The figures from the census also show the numbers of houses by townland.

Housing Statistics	1821	1831	1841	1851	1861	1871	1881
Abbey Parish							
Abbey East			3	2	1	1	1
Abbey West			18	11	14	14	12
Ailwee			1	1	2	1	1
Ballyhehan			17	12	7	8	8
Ballyvelaghan			45	55	79	61	58
Cartron			3	2	1	1	1
Currenrue			24	15	15	11	11
Dooneen			22	18	18	17	17
Moneen			4	1	1	1	1
Mortyclough			16	10	10	6	6
Munnia			61	18	18	12	11
Rossalia			12	2	5	5	4
Sheshia			6	6	7	7	6
Creg Town				22			
Total Abbey			**230**	**152**	**176**	**154**	**142**
Oughtmama							
Aughawinnan			17	12	8	7	9
Aughinish			3	3	29	24	22

Beagh			12	5	5	7	6
Cragbally-conell			1	2	2	1	1
Deelin Beg			16	1	2	3	1
Deelin Mor			4	1	1	2	2
Finavara Demesne			3	2	4	2	2
Gortboyheen			7	1	1	3	3
Gortaclare			18	7	14	8	8
Kilweelran			17	5	5	4	5
Knockycallan			4	2	2	3	3
New Quay			28	9	18	21	18
Oughtmama			20	15	11	12	11
poulaphuca			1	1	1	2	2
Rine			2	10	46	38	35
Slievecarran			2	1	1	1	1
Turlough			74	39	30	31	27
Aughinish Town			45	29			
Finavarra Town			54	45			
Total Oughtmama			**328**	**192**	**200**	**169**	**156**
Total Abbey & Oughtmama	**0**	**0**	**558**	**344**	**376**	**323**	**298**

Table 2. 19th century Housing Statistics by Parish/Townland

An analysis of the condition of the houses in the census of 1841, gives an indication of the extent of poverty.

Area	1st Class	2nd Class	3rd Class	4th Class	Un-inhabited	Total	4th Class as % of Total
Abbey Total	1	37	65	120	7	230	52%
Oughtmama Rural	1	20	45	161	2	229	70%

Aughinish Town		2	21	22		45	49%
Finavarra Town		3	19	31		53	58%
Total Houses	2	62	150	334	9	557	60%

Table 3. 19th century Housing by Class

Houses were graded into 4 classes, the 4th and lowest class consisted of windowless, cabins, often made of mud with a single room. The high percentage living in this category emphasises the wretched conditions of a high proportion of the population.

Legacy of The Famine

To the observer in the years after the famine, New Quay was once again prosperous, as the gentry returned to spend the summer season, sea bathing at the Flaggy Shore. The bones and DNA of the un-coffined bodies, victims of the famine, decayed into the earth in the overcrowded churchyards, forgotten, as according to Rev Coffey, their numbers were too numerous to record. While the 1851 census included a report of the numbers of deaths in the preceding years, the information was collected from the heads of households who recorded deaths occurring in their families but there was no one to account for the dead for entire families who were obliterated by death, disease, emigration or moving to the workhouse. Many of those who could, like my great granduncle Patrick Fawle, emigrated, taking the boat, as he did in 1851 from Galway to New York. Today, no physical evidence of deserted famine villages exists, no mass graveyards or memorials survives as testimony of the destitution and heartbreak of its people.

Section 2.
History of Places,
Names and Origins

3. The Tale of New Quay Placenames History and Origin

Background

When many of the historical markers and evidence have been lost, bulldozed, or obliterated from the landscape, we are often left with just the old names, names of townlands, fields, mountains, and streams which give us clues to their places in history and the lives and beliefs of the people who lived there. Deciphering the original meanings of those names can shed light on the history and early peoples who have often left no traces except through the place names.

Charles II clearly wasn't a fan of Irish placenames. In 1665, during his reign, new laws were enacted in Ireland to ensure according to the statutes, that *"new and proper names more suitable to the English tongue may be inserted with an alias for all towns, lands and places in that kingdom"* This was a response to; *"his majesty taking note of the barbarous and uncouth names by which most of the towns and places in this Kingdom of Ireland are called."* This was the beginning of the anglicisation of Irish place names. It was usual to follow the phonetic pronunciation which lost much of the original meaning whilst also dropping alternative names by which places had previously been known. We can get a glimpse of the names as they were anglicised in the 17th century from the Books of Survey and Distribution (BSD). These books were compiled in the 1670's and provide a list of the townlands, including acreage and proportions of profitable and unprofitable land within each parish, by barony and county. They include the proprietors in 1641 and the new landlords to whom the land was transferred after the upheavals of the Cromwellian Wars and the subsequent restoration of the monarchy under Charles II.

The next major review of placenames took place under the Ordnance Survey of Ireland completed between 1824 and 1842. This survey was undertaken to establish townlands and boundaries for land valuations and land tax purposes. A team of officers from the British Army were sent to complete detailed maps of the whole country. Part of the work included creating English versions of the names of townlands that phonetically resembled the commonly used names in Irish. The names of townlands in English decided then are largely in use still today. Along the way, names got lost or corrupted through translation and amalgamation and quite often we can only guess at the true origin by unravelling the elements of a placename. P.W. Joyce (1827 –1914) was an Irish historian and scholar whose pioneering work on investigations into the origin of Irish placenames examines the names, sources, meaning and make up of Irish placenames. His extensive research provides the basis for much of what we know today as to why and how townlands got their names.

Corker Hill

One such name is Corker Hill. Located on the boundaries of Connaught and Munster, for hundreds of years Corker

Hill has been an important gateway between Galway and Clare. Important as a trade route, there are also numerous references in the annals of forays by invaders and enemies, stories of the kings of Connaught and Thomond and the local lords, Ui Fiachrach Aidhne of South Galway, and the Corco Modruadh of North Clare, using the route to attack and returning with hostages, booty, and cattle. The annals mention Red Hugh O'Donnell, Chief of the O'Donnells and Lord of Tirconnell, travelling this route with his men in 1599, on his way home through Connaught having plundered Clare. The annals record that the devastation was such that all the country behind and around them was enveloped in smoke. As his men rode through Corcaigh na Cleirigh they were barely able to find their way through the thick smoke arising from the burning countryside they had left in their wake.

The name, anglicised as Corker Hill, or in Irish Corcaigh na Cleirigh, is translated from the Latin Carcer de Clericorum. One of only a handful of Irish place names which are Latin in origin, it suggests the name dates from a time when Latin was the everyday language as spoken by the Cistercian monks who lived in nearby Corcomroe Abbey. The literal translation of Carcer de Clericorum is the "Clerics Prison" or place where the clerics were incarcerated. The rule of St Benedict, written in 516 A.D., from which all monastic rules including the Cistercian Rule trace their origin, required each monastery to punish monks who committed misdemeanours. A separate place, the *Carcer de Clericorum,* a prison cell, was to be set aside for the incarceration of monks. Today there is no trace of a cell in the landscape and in modern times the name Carcer de Clericorum has been translated as meaning the "Narrow Pass of the Cleric" in reference to the pass between the mountains, where the monks would have trod on their way to the coast.

Today the physical evidence of New Quay's monastic past, lies in the splendid ruins of Corcomroe Abbey, and the three churches at Oughtmama, once the homes of communities of monks which thrived over a period of nearly 1000 years. Yet their legacy lives also in the names of places they dominated. Corcomroe Abbey founded in the early 12th century was selected as a place where the monks could live far from human society and remote from the dwellings of secular men in line with the Cistercian values. Places which at the time the abbey was founded were considered isolated and inaccessible. Yet the monks were also fishermen and farmers and traders. The lands that are still today Abbey electoral division, constituting about half of New Quay parish, were historically in the hands of the Cistercians. Corcomroe Abbey and Oughtmama are situated in the valley known as Glennamannagh (Gleann na Manach, translates as the valley of the monks). In 17th century documents the whole parish of Abbey and Oughtmama is referred to as Gleann na Manach.

Near Turlough in the district of Oughtmama there is a townland called Kilweelran. This is marked in the Book of Survey and Distributions as Kilmoylan alias Kilmulran. Local folklore has it that following the dissolution of the monasteries, when the Cistercian monks were driven from the abbey they moved here and built a hut to live in and as a place of prayer. The site became a graveyard and was still used as a cillin where local people buried unbaptised children up until the 1930's. In Irish the townland Kilweelran can be translated as Cill O' Maoláin, the Church of Moylan or the church of the bald headed or tonsured one. and the name O' Maoláin was often applied to monastic sites or those associated with monks.

In old maps and documents, dating from the 16th century the coastal strip of land in front of Munnia and Rossalia is identified as Carrowillian or Carrowanweelaun. While the name is no longer used today the origin can be interpreted as Carrow O Maoláin, which phonetically matches, meaning the quarter of the bald headed or tonsured one i.e., the Monks quarter. Carcer de Clericorum, (modern day Corker pass) links the abbey to Carrowillian, on the coast. The rule forbade Cistercians from eating meat, so fish was central to the monastic diet and everywhere they went the Cistercian secured rights to fish and fisheries. The oyster beds around Munnia and Aughinish Bay would have been an important source of foods for the Corcomroe monks. The Cistercian rules required each abbey to be fully self-sufficient, and this self-sufficiency was achieved by setting up monastic farms which were known as granges, managed by the Conversi i.e., lay monks. The Cistercians were an enclosed order which meant the monks had to stay within the grounds of the abbey, but the lay monks were allowed to travel within a day's journey from the abbey, to work. While today we know for sure that Corcomroe Abbey was the spiritual home, the ecclesiastical remains at Rossalia, (identified as Gardeen Rossalia in early Ordnance Survey maps from 1842), could indicate that there was once a grange here. An old map from 1605 (see below), preserved in the British Library suggests this site had monastic ties.

8. Extract of 1605 Map of Abbey and Oughtmama preserved in the British Library

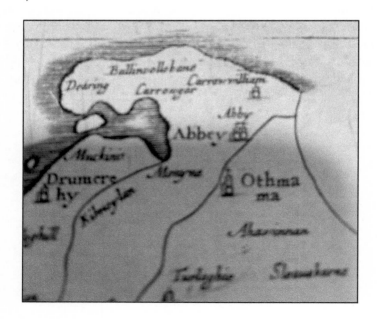

9. Down Survey Map of 1670 showing a building with cross in Rossalia

In the 1840's Ordnance Survey maps, the structure is shown in the place called Gardeen Rossalia and contained the ruins of a stone building. By then it was used as the site of a cillin with a small, enclosed wall to the front. To the right is the location of what then was the village of Rossalia. The cillin was in use up until the early 20th century. These cillins or children's cemeteries were primarily used for the burial of children who died before being baptised. According to church doctrine, unbaptised children would be unable to enter heaven and could not be buried in consecrated ground. Perhaps the local priests turned a blind eye to bereaved parents who brought their tiny bundles here for secret burial. My father told me of his still-born sister, taken here for burial in the 1910's. The burials were performed in secret and happened after dark.

Cillins can be found all over Ireland. 136 have been identified in Clare, 3 of which are in the parish of New Quay (formerly Abbey and Oughtmama). These are in Turlough, Rossalia and Aughinish. Cillins are quite often found close to the sea or near borders of townlands and in the sites of former ecclesiastical buildings. Those who had taken their own lives or women who died having recently given birth and were unchurched, also suffered the same fate as unbaptised children, and were buried in cillins. From today's perspective it seems a cruel fate for the families with strong Catholic beliefs that their departed relatives could not be buried in consecrated grounds and were denied heaven. The field at Rossalia has since been cleared and all that remains now is the ruins of the stone building.

The lands around Rossalia and Munnia remained abbey lands until they reverted to the Earl of Thomond under Henry VIII. But the electoral division and civil parish name of Abbey survives, tracing its boundaries back to the lands granted by the O'Brien kings to the Cistercians 800 years ago.

Rossalia and Munnia

The townland of Rosalia lies to the west of Corker Hill. Ros is translated sometimes as a wood and sometimes a headland. Aila (short for saile) means salty so Rosalia can be translated as the salty wood or headland. In the Book of Survey and Distributions the townland, is called Rosraily and in deeds of the Inchiquin estates from the early 18th century the townland is referred to as Rossrawley. According to Joyce's analysis of Irish place Rail or Ral (rawl) is another term for an oak tree. Ly or ley means 'abounding in' so Rosrawley, the earlier name, can be translated as the "Wood abounding in oaks" or the "Oak Wood".

In 1713, in a dispute over a lease of lands (in trust for Lucius O'Brien), between William, the Earl of Inchiquin and Alderman Twigge, Twigge complained about the inaccessibility of the lands in Rossrawley, from the evidence his agent provided:

> *"These lands that lie near the Western Ocean are in a very remote and wild country scarcely inhabited except by a few shepherds and are many miles from any public road passable for a carriage and without any decent habitation and when the agent tried to visit the said lands he was obliged to walk a great part of the way there and found the lands to be nearly in a state of nature. He didn't believe that the proprietor or the principal tenant had resided there for the last 50 years and said it was impossible to determine the boundaries. He deduced that the land had been held in common."*

Further west from Rossalia lies the townland of Munnia. Munnia is sometimes said to be derived from Muine, the Irish for shrubbery, but in his analysis of place names, Joyce also refers to derivation from mbun where the b gets eclipsed in the old Irish pronunciation (in force between 10th and 15th centuries). Mbun, meaning "base" or "foot of", refers to the location of the original village of Munnia nestling at the base of Abbey Hill or what was earlier called Beha Hill. The BSD shows that these townlands were in the hands of Lord Inchiquin in 1641 and retained by him after the re-settlement. Being resident in England and a Protestant, he did not require a Decree of Innocence to retain the lands after the Restoration resettlements in 1654.

The townland of Munnia covered not just the village but all the land extending down the Bealach Duine (translated as the steep pass) to the lakes. In the census reports of the 19th century, Munnia included the inhabitants of Lisovane. The Tithe records of the 1820's shows 9 families living in the village of Lisovane who were obliged to pay tithes. The name Lisovane, is composed of two parts or root words. *Lios* were early settlements, a type of ringfort i.e.an earthen or stone enclosure. There are different ways to interpret the second part of the name "vane" which could come from ban, the Irish for white, or bawn a field or a place where cows were kept. The custom of housing cows in the home was practised throughout Europe in the early medieval period and Ireland was no exception. While the remnants of many ringforts can still be seen in the landscape, the evidence for Lisovane ringfort and village has completely disappeared.

The hill to the west of Munnia is known as Lisovane Hill and it has its place in history. In 1831 Lisovane Hill was the site of a battle, when a large gathering of Terry Alts took on the forces of the crown in a skirmish on the summit. The Terry Alts were members of a secret society in Clare, one of many set up to fight against unjust rent, clearances, access to common land and payment of tithes to the Protestant Church. The price of wheat and crops had fallen dramatically after the end of the Napoleonic Wars and landowners switched from crops to grazing land for cattle in the 1820s. Many of the labourers and small farmers who previously rented land for growing potatoes under the conacre system lost their land and livelihood as the land previously used for tillage, where each small farmer was allocated a strip of land for tillage, was now turned into pasture. The Terry Alts mainly engaged in terror attacks at night against those they saw as the enemy, including landowners but also smaller farmers who had replaced the original owners. The protests included levelling of walls and maiming of cattle as well as arson attacks and assault and digging up of pasture lands. A hole in the shape of a coffin was often dug outside the houses as a warning to those seen as the enemy.

Cartron

The name Cartron is derived from the Anglo Norman signifying a quarter of land, approximately 30 acres. In the BSD of the 1670's, the townland was in the possession of Robert Dixon. Robert Dixon was on the list of Adventurers, i.e., those granted lands instead of payment in return for providing military service during the Cromwellian wars. While Captain Browne is listed as the tithe payer for Cartron in the 1820's tithes, Cartron House or lodge was the holiday home of Bindon Scott of Cahircon and landlord in the Burren. Contemporary newspaper society columns announced the arrival of the gentry, including Bindon Scott and Daniel O Connell for the Summer season to New Quay in the 1830's. Scott maintained a yacht in New Quay where in the Summer he organised Regattas with Daniel O Connell as the judge. In 1838 the *Dublin Register* published:

> *"Observer at New Quay, County Clare, Oct. 11, 1838. —The last of the ephemeral inhabitants of this nice little bathing place leave us tomorrow. But the departure of temporary visitors may well dispense with, until the returning summer shall recall their appearance on this wild coast, while Mrs. Scott, of Cahircon, the mother-in-law of Mr. Maurice O'Connell, shall continue to sojourn in her*

elegantly fitted up and hospitable lodge, Cartron. Mr Scott's beautiful yacht, the Emerald, is staying at the quay here. We had a delightful cruise in it with Mrs. Scott to Galway, yesterday, and returned through the foaming element with "snoring breeze," after partaking of sumptuous déjeuner onboard, in the Galway roads. This day the sea tuns high here, and the weather looks wild, but the barometer stands fair still."

In 1839, following the death of Bindon Scott, the contents of Cartron House were put up for auction and a year later the house was sold. The description of the contents in the auction catalogue provides a stark contrast between the opulence enjoyed by the gentry and the lives of the poor in this period, when 75% of the parish lived in one roomed cabin. The auction describes the house contents for sale as follows:

"CARTRON HOUSE – Burren Auction. Of very Elegant Household Furniture, China, Glass, a Suite of Superb Plated Wares, House Linen, Joseph James Marshall are favoured with instruction to Sell by Auction, Cartron

HOUSE, NEW-QUAY. BURREN, the entire of the Elegant Furniture and contents. It has all been purchased from the most respectable Cabinet Makers in Ireland, within a few months, and comprises every article of the best description and fashion that good taste could suggest.

In the parlour are the usual requisites of the most substantial kind —Chairs, Set Tables, Dumb Waiter, Fenders, Fire Irons, elegant Gard vine and Tea Store, Oil Cloth, with Carpet Covering, Crimson and Maroon Window Curtains.

The drawing room contains Mahogany Chairs, covered in rich Chintz, to correspond with the Window Curtains, which are tastefully hung; Swiss Chairs in Rosewood, Sofas, Loungers, Easy Chairs, Corner Chairs, Priers, Pier Cabinet large Crimson Screen, handsome Round Table, with Cover, beautiful Painted Centre Round Table, Writing Tables, Work, Music Waggon, Book

Rack, Verd Antique Row-leaf Vases, Carpet Hearth Rug, Bronze Fender, Fire Brasses, Pendule Clock. The China, Glass, and Plated Services, all of which are extremely handsome.

The bedrooms contain elegant 4 Post Mahogany Bedsteads, with Chintz Curtains; best Hair Mattresses, superior Feather Beds, Bolsters Down Pillows, Blankets, of the finest description House Linen, comprising immense quantity of Fine Sheeting, Tablecloths, Napkins, Towels and Overlays; Dressing Glasses, Basin Stands, Commodes, Dressing Table, beside Stands, Shoe Racks, Clothes, Horses. Chests of Drawers, Wardrobes, all the first-class Mahogany; Window Curtains, Fenders, Fire Guards, Fire Irons, Chamber Ware, Room, and Stair Carpeting.

The Second-Class bedrooms contain French Bedsteads and Hangings, Hair Mattresses, Best Feather Beds, Bolsters, Pillows, Blanketing, Bedding, Chamber Ware, Basin Stands, Commodes, Bidets, Dressing Glasses, Dressing Tables, Presses, Fenders, Fire Irons, Chest of Drawers, Curtains, Footbaths, Round Tables, Carpeting.

The servant's hall and sleeping rooms are fully furnished. The hall contains a capital Clock, Cloth, Flower Stand, Hall Chairs, Large Mahogany Table, Office Table, Clothes Backs,

Also included a quantity of Room Paper, 3 Inch Shoots, Watering Cart, a pair of handsome Ponies, 3 years old, with Double Harness."

In the 1840's the Persse family of Roxborough acquired the leasehold and Cartron House became their holiday home. As a child Lady Gregory would have spent her summers in Cartron along with her numerous siblings. The freehold of the land and house was the property of the Brady Brownes and from the late 19th century the family retained the house as a holiday home for their own use. The Brady and Browne families were tied through intermarriage and continued to own the house until the 1930's when it fell into ruin. The Madden family were listed in the Tithe records and Griffith Valuation as domestic servants and caretakers of

Cartron House in the 19th century. The Madden family purchased the land under the tenant land purchase schemes in the early 20th century. Mary Madden who lived all her life in the shadow of Cartron House, recalled visits of the Brady Brownes in the summer season, and the dances Mrs Brady Browne held in the drawing room in the 1920's for local people. In the 1990's, following the death of Mary and her brother Paddy Madden, what remained of the ruins of Cartron House was knocked to make way for new homes.

In front of Cartron lies a small island called Illaunacoran translated as Island of the weir, ford, or steppingstones. According to Joyce a weir across a river either for fishing or to divert a stream is called in Irish Cora or Coran. Could the name have been derived from a man-made weir across Aughinish Bay?

Aughinish

The island of Aughinish although linked by a causeway to Doorus in County Galway has been part of Clare since records began and from at least the 14th century it has formed part of the parish of Oughtmama. Local folklore tells that the island of Aughinish was physically linked to Clare before the Lisbon earthquake of 1755. On the morning of the 1st of November of that year, an earthquake struck Lisbon and by the end of the week almost 100,000 people had died making this one of the deadliest natural disasters Europe has ever experienced. The day marked the Feast of All Saints, and the churches were packed. As the tremors struck the churches toppled and packed with candles (lit in honour of the feast day), huge fires started that raged across the city for five days. The Royal Family was not in its Lisbon palace when the earthquake occurred. It is said that the king afterwards would not reside in any building, such was his claustrophobia caused by the earthquake and instead enormous tents had to be erected for him to stay in as he travelled. The earthquake was followed by a massive tsunami that raged along the Atlantic coast and was even felt in Brazil the other side of the ocean. In Ireland it caused massive structural damage all along the coast. The giant, powerful waves tore through Aughinish Bay, causing deep chasms in the seabed and knocking everything in their way including toppling Hynes Castle at the head of the bay at Currenrue. However, the evidence from documents tells a different story. Early maps predating 1755 show that Aughinish was already an island. While the earthquake and subsequent tsunami was not the cause of the separation of Aughinish from the mainland, it seems likely that it did destroy an existing low-lying connection between Aughinish and New Quay. Whether this was a natural ford, or a man-made crossing, "stepping-stones," we cannot know for sure.

As with many other places, evidence can often be found in the placename. The BSD spells the name as Aghinis and deeds from the early 1700's show that the island was known as Agh Inis. Using Joyce's analysis, Agh often stands for Ath (ah) a ford, sometimes Agh and Agha means a field, but sometimes it is derived from Each, a young horse. Today the usual translation for Aughinish is the island of the young horse. However, with the evidence of fords, a more accurate interpretation of its origins is possibly *Island of the fords*, with one ford being the site of the current causeway that links to Doorus and an earlier one at Cartron (before the tsunami that cleared the intertidal crossing). Another clue is in the name "Gaeth" According to O'Donovan gaeth was an old Irish word for estuary where there was *"a shallow stream into which the tide flows and is fordable at low water"*. Next to the causeway that links Doorus and Aughnish there are two townlands, called respectively Gaeth North and Gaeth South. The hill at the back of Cartron is also called Knocnagaeth and the fields next to the Cartron shoreline are still known as "Gaeth Dearg". So, as well as a ford on the Clare side, the link between Aughinish and Doorus was probably also fordable or crossable at low tide before the tsunami struck.

One can only imagine the shock felt by the residents of Aughinish when they woke up the morning after the tsunami to find out that they were cut off and could no longer walk across the bay to reach other parts of Clare. For the next 50 years Aughinish remained an island until a causeway was built in 1810, to give the British garrison access to a new Martello Tower built in Aughinish (as a defence in case of a French invasion). The causeway linked, and still links today, Aughinish to Doorus in the county of Galway.

The island of Aughinish was split into four ceathru or quarters. Three of those were called Ceathru an Tobar (the quarter of the well), Ceathru na H'aille (the quarter of the cliffs), and Ceathru an Bruim Fhead (the quarter of the long grass or couch grass.), all of which get their names from features of the land or landscape. The fourth quarter was known as Ceathru Droim Breathnach. Droim was an area of marshy land while Breathnach is the Irish version of the surname Walsh. But in Gaelic Ireland Breathnach also refers to a Welshman or a foreigner of Norman descent from England or Normandy. In the early 19th century, the French family, of Norman descent, rented Aughinish from the Bishop of Killaloe. The BSD shows that the Protestant Bishop of Killaloe was the landowner for Aughinish in 1641 and retained the lands after the restoration. The French family may have been the "breathnach" or foreigners after which the fourth quarter was named.

Aughinish had its own church, the ruins of which are gradually being eroded by sea. In her book Forgotten Stones describing the church ruins of the Burren, Averil Swinfen refers to a date 1617, carved on the outside of the north wall of the church in Aughinish. It is not known what this date refers to. Coincidentally 1617 was the year that the Diocese of Kilfenora came under the Diocese of Tuam. Sinead Ni Ghabhlain in her thesis on the churches of Kilfenora diocese estimates that the church was built in the $11^{th}/12^{th}$ century based on the fabric of the stonework, the same period as the second and third church of Oughtmama. Like most churches from this period, the church was probably built on the site of an earlier ecclesiastical site. Evidence of part of the original enclosure can still be deciphered in the landscape. In early medieval times, churches were often built near territory boundaries and Aughinish would have occupied the furthest corner of Thomond, under the O'Briens. It was also church lands, with the landlord being the Bishop of Killaloe, another feature common to lands on the borders of territories. According to Avril Swinfen the church was known locally as the Ullord Church. Ullord, she translates as orchard. The church, with just one room was probably a "chapel of ease" used by the parish priest of New Quay to say Mass, saving the people of Aughinish the longer journey to the parish church at Oughtmama or later Dooneen.

Ballyvelaghan

Ballyvelaghan comes from the Irish *Baile Beal an Lachan* literally translates as the place or town at the mouth of the small lake or stream. The townland of Ballyvelaghan extended from Cartron to Rhodesia House. In early 19th century Fisheries Board documentation, the stretch of water between present day New Quay and Aughinish was often referred to as the Burren stream. The derivation of Lachan as a translation of a small stream, could be derived from the townland location in front of Aughinish. But it could also have got its name from the lakes nearby. In the BSD and old deeds from the 17th and 18th century, the townland was also known as Ballydonnell translated as Donal or Daniel's place. In 1641 the landowners here were Turlogh Mor O'Loughlin,

Owen Leisagh O'Loughlin and William Neylon, all under the lordship of the Earl of Thomond. In the BSD of the 1670's, the Earl of Inchiquin (the Earl of Thomond's new title), is listed as the landowner. The O'Loughlin's lands had been forfeited, but William Neylon retained title to the lands. Robert Dixon who owned Cartron after the restoration was also given lands in Ballyvelaghan.

New Quay forms part of Ballyvelaghan townland. When the quay was built on the current site in the 1820's, a place called New Quay already existed. According to Alexander Nimmo, (the Scottish engineer who was responsible for the design along with some 28 other quays around Galway Bay) the site was the third attempt to build a quay in the area. Earlier sites were further to the west, closer to Rhodesia House. The landowners of Ballyvelaghan and New Quay from the late 18th century, were the Scott family of Cahircon until after the famine when the land was purchased by William Lane Joynt agent for Baron Annaly.

In 1838 John Scott placed the following advertisement in the Limerick Chronicle:

"To be let from the first of May for such terms as may be agreed upon, PLOTS of GROUND for building, at the New Quay, BURREN, which is known for its celebrity bathing place, and where every facility presents itself for the amusement of Yachting and Boating. One of these plots will be let on moderate terms for the site of a hotel, and some of the necessary materials can be had on the spot Apply John Bindon Scott, Esq. Cahircon, or to William Cannon, Esq. his Agent, Cottage, Kildysart."

The site for the hotel later became known as Rhodesia House.

Balycuneen

Balycuneen – Baile a choinín, translates as the "Place of the Rabbits." It is said to get its name from the numerous rabbits found here. In old deeds the placename is marked as alias Cuan meaning quay, or Cuaneen the diminutive, meaning small quay. This is the site of the old quay, close by the beach at the Flaggy Shore which was in use until sometime in the 19th century. Ballycuaneen, the place of the small quay is the most likely translation from the earlier name which got corrupted to Balycuneen.

Finavarra

Finavarra to the west of New Quay has one of the oldest placenames in the parish. It gets a mention in the life of St Patrick, the Vita Tripartita written around the 10th century. The authors state that the territories of the Dal Cais, ancestors of the O'Briens and the first kings of Munster, stretched as far north as Fidnach Bira in the Burren. The Dal Cais were the overlords of the Corco Modruadh by the end of the first millennium. The Corco Modruadh were the local chieftains whose territory was Corcomroe, (named after them) but which at the time combined both the baronies of the Burren and Corcomroe. There are several interpretations of what the name Finavarra means and how it was derived.

Fionaigh Bheara in Irish could be translated as the wood of Beara. According to one version the name comes from Beara, a member of the tribe of the Fir Bolg. In Irish medieval myth, the Fir Bolg were one of six races that in earlier times invaded and ruled Ireland. According to mythology they were driven west to Connaught to seek refuge from Queen Maebh when Ireland was taken over by the Tuatha de Danann. They were reputed to have settled around the south and east of Galway Bay. One of them 'Aenghus' went to Inis More in the Aran Islands and built Dun Aenghus, Cutra settled in Lough Cutra and Beara settled in the place that became known as Fionaigh Bheara or Finavarra.

Other mythologies say Finavarra was the king of the Sidhe, the fairies, the remnants of the Tuatha de Danann who were driven underground when Ireland was taken over by the Milesians. The fairies were believed to occupy ring forts which were also known as fairy forts. The ring forts, built between 500 and 1200 AD were left untouched for centuries for fear of reprisals for interfering with the fairy world. Stories tell that Finavarra, the king of the fairies, held court in the glens of Ireland before settling in the fairy fort at Knockmoy near Tuam in Galway.

The 19th century antiquarian Cooke provides his own interpretation of the name Finavarra in the Autumnal Rambles around New Quay. *"The name seems to be more properly traceable to the circumstance of its having been the locality where the Brehon held his sittings. Finne signifies, attendance testimony and Beara is a judge. The Four Masters (ad an. 1514) spell the name Finagh-Beara."* Considering the historic context, beside the locality of the O'Dalaigh bardic school, Cooke's interpretation would appear to hold most weight.

The Earl of Thomond was identified as the owner in 1641 although there exist separate deeds to show that Teige O'Dalys and Martin Lynch of Galway had leases. After the Cromwellian resettlements, the land, along with the townland of Rine and Scanlan Island, came into the ownership of Carey Dillon. Colonel Carey Dillon was a Protestant nobleman and professional soldier. He had supplied his army of soldiers, cavalry, and equipment for the subjugation of Ireland under Cromwell in return for payment or the promise of lands confiscated. Cromwell's famous edict 'to hell or to Connaught' meant that all the lands east of the Shannon were reserved for Protestants and the English settlers and adventurers, while all the original Irish, 'the innocent papists' who had not taken up arms were transplanted to Clare and Connaught. Untrusting of the Irish settlers and fearful of attacks from the sea, the rules stipulated that the transplanted Irish could not hold land within a mile of the west coast or the river Shannon. The lands on the coastline from Sligo to the Shannon estuary and all along the Shannon were allocated to the English adventurers and soldiers in lieu of the arrears owing to them from the war effort. The records in the BSD for 1671 show that many of the townlands close by the sea in the Burren and Kinvara, including Doorus, Rineen, Finavarra, Rine, and Scanlan Island and present day Ballyvaughan were after the transplantations the property of Colonel Cary Dillon. He received the lands in Clare and Galway under the mile-wide rule. Many of the solders and adventurers soon sold the lands acquired, unable or unwilling to rebuild after the devastation caused by the Cromwellian soldiers and fearful of attack from those whose homes and lands had been destroyed. The will of James Skerrett of Galway shows that he purchased the land in Finavarra from Carey Dillon in the 1680's.

The name Finavarra doesn't get a mention in the BSD, Instead, the area is referred to as Dearing alias Derreen alias Ballaknavin. Using Joyce's derivations Deáring is the corruption of Doire Na Aenach, which literally means oak wood of the assembly or fair. Derreen can be translated as Doire Rine oak wood of the spit. But the strangest derivation of all is Ballaknavin.In Irish Baile Na Cnaimhin the place of the small bones!

The O'Dalaigh, poets to O'Loughlins ran a bardic school in Finavarra from the 13th century. In the Inquisition of 1622 when James 1st granted the Earl of Thomond permission to hold 6 manor courts in Thomond, where English Common Law would be administrated, Finavarra (Manerium de Flyn Ivarra) was the site of one of those Manor Courts. The O'Loughlins, (chieftains of the Burren from the 11th/12th century) had a castle in Finavarra although no trace of it remains today.

In his trips to Finavarra in the 1830's Cooke explored the ringfort called Lios Boireann. Within the fort was a souterrain (an underground passage), in which he found a chamber with what resembled a stone alter, a flat flagstone on four upright stones with bones underneath. He concluded that this was an ancient sepulchre i.e., a burial place for some once great and long forgotten leader. Evidence from numerous other sites that were places of assembly in early Irish history show that tribes gathered in hills and mountains that were also places of burials of ancestral leaders.

Ringforts

Between 500 and 1000 AD, ringforts were the most common type of settlement in Ireland. They consisted of one or more houses inside an enclosure of stone or earthen banks. The outer banks were designed to protect the inhabitants from wild animals but also from attacks by those trying to steal cattle. Many of the ringforts also had souterrains, as places of storage but also a means of escape in case of an attack. The antiquarian Westropp in his study of the forts in Clare remarked that those around New Quay in their structure resembled more closely those of Galway and Meath, compared to the rest of Clare. This may be due that up until the 8th century, this part of the Burren was under the control of the Adhne branch of the Ui Fiachrach who ruled over South Galway. From the 8th century the Dal Cais (ancestors of the O'Briens), drove them out and the Dal Cais in turn became overlords of the Corco Modruadh the local chieftains. The Corco Modruadh, (seeds of Ruadh), claimed descent from the mythical Fergus Mac Roich. According to the Táin Bó Cúailnge, an epic tale from the Ulster cycles, Fergus had been King of Ulster, who, when he was forced into exile, became the lover of Queen Maebh of Connaught. Together they had three sons, one of whom was Modruadh. Modruadh settled in North Clare and with his descendants became the local kings and gave Corcomroe (from Corcomruadh), its name. The descendants later split into two septs, taking the surnames O'Loughlin and O'Connor.

Although it is hundreds of years since they were in use, traces of ringforts are still very much in existence in the landscape today. What we tend to find is one ringfort for each townland and although evidence of who the inhabitants were has long disappeared, it is an indication of the long-lasting existence of the townland, analogous with one per extended family or kin group from ancient times. Parkmore or An Pháirc Mhór in Irish, is translated as the large field or enclosure. The name Parc often referred to demesne lands granted to the hereditary poets of a chieftain, in this case the O'Dalaighs who had a school close by. Parkmore contains the remains of a ringfort dating from the first millennium. Mortyclough is derived from Mhothar Ti Cloch, the ruins of the stone house. Moher means the ruins or site of a settlement or enclosure. The place is also mentioned in the Inchiquin Manuscripts from the 17th century and pronounced Magherteiloghy, which is the plain or field of the stone house. The remains of two ringforts are still here, one was identified as much older by Westropp which had remains of stone instead of an earthen enclosure. The place-name Dooneen, is translated as the small dune or ringfort. In an old map of 1608 Cahir Doon is identified and the doon or fort remains are still evident close by New Quay church today. The remains of a ringfort exist on Scanlan's Island (translates as Oileán na gCaorach – the island of the sheepfold) and one called Gortagreenaun (translates as the field of the Summer House) in Rine. The road to Corcomroe Abbey cuts through an old ringfort. It is not known if the road dates to the arrival of the Cistercians and whether the ringfort settlers were evicted when the O'Briens granted the land to the monks, or if the road traversing the ringfort was built in later years. The Catholic clergy often built churches on old ringforts as an expression of their disapproval and opposition to the pisreogs, superstitions and customs associated with the fairy forts.

Booleying

There is a long tradition of booleying or transhumance in Irish history from the Gaelic times. The practice involved moving cattle from the lowlands or more fertile ground to higher or rougher grazing during the Spring and Summer season. This allowed crops and grass to grow undisturbed in the arable lands before cattle were moved back in autumn and winter for grazing and to fertilise the land. In earlier times, members of the family, usually the women responsible for milking, moved with the cattle, living in basic huts known as clachans before all moving back at the end of the harvest. Perversely in the Burren, the practise, which continues today, involved moving the cattle to the mountain and limestone areas in the winter. The nature of the limestone meant that grass and herbs between the rock fissures was rich for winter grazing and hollows in the rocks were a source of rainwater while in much of the Burren the land in the lowlands was waterlogged in winter by the turloughs and underground streams. The townland of Turlough takes its name from the lakes that are formed from underground streams in winter.

The custom of booleying lives on in the local place names. The Irish word Buaile is translated as a feeding or milking place for cows and usually can be identified as a place for those temporary houses. At the back of Cartron Hill there is a place known as Shawnwalla or Sean Buaile, the old booley. At the edge of the mountain, it had been the site of a village until the Irish famine, and after the famine, those that survived and did not emigrate moved to Cregg, beside the lakes at Ballyvelaghan. But the name was in use for centuries before the famine years. According to Joyce, 'sean', the Irish word for old, when part of a place name usually meant very old, as in use from ancient times. In the tithe records the land here on Cartron Hill was identified as common land, although by then, the village would have been in use for permanent settlement due to population pressures on those seeking out a living from marginal land. Shawnvally in Oughtmama townland also derives its name from a derivation of Sean Buaile, the old booley. In a Spring visit to Oughtmama in 1895, Lord Dunravan described watching the local women.

> *"In the early morning the women bring their milk pails on their heads may be seen ascending the mountain with free elastic step and their voices heard across the hills as they call their cows to their side for milking. The red and purple dresses of the women, the cattle, the green pasture form strong and delightful contrasts of colour to the grey tones of the scene." (Notes on Irish Architecture – Lord Dunraven 1895)*

The evidence for a long history of grazing on the mountains is manifested in the stone walls that stretch up the mountains, often marking boundaries between townlands. On the Galway Bay side of Abbey Hill, a stretch of stone walls goes to the top separating Munnia from Beagh townland. The grazing rights would have been shared by the tenants of a townland. Earlier, in the BSD, the townland of Beagh (translated as the place of the birch trees but can also sometimes be derived from Beaghan translates as the feeding place), was identified as part owned by Abbey Parish and in part by Oughtmama but the boundaries could not be ascertained suggesting that the land here around Abbey Hill, (known then as Beagh Hill), and in other townlands with mountainous uplands for grazing, was then in common use.

The estate records for the sale of the Bindon estate in Munnia and Rossalia show that in the 1850's while the practise of holding land in common had disappeared, the system of rundale was still in use, whereby two or more tenant farmers paid rent to share the grazing rights for some mountainous lands.

Bellharbour

The quay at Bellharbour, known by the name Beal na Cloigheann, gets frequent mention in the annals. It translates as the Mouth of the Skull. While there are lots of references to Beal na Cloigheann in the wars over the sovereignty of Clare from the 11th century, the cloigheann meaning skull, refers to the round headed mountain tops that surround the quay rather than any mass casualties from old battles.

Scaghbreeda

Scaghbreeda translates as Bridget's Bush. This refers to the site of a hawthorn bush, described as a "holy tree" which was the site of worship and prayer for centuries. Bridget is said to refer to Saint Bridget of Kildare, whose feast day is 1st February. the beginning of Spring. However, Briga was also the mother of St Mac Creiche who was the patron saint and kinsman of the Corco Modruadh the chieftains of North Clare in the second half of the first millennium.

Currenrue

The townland of Currenrue lies on the border of Clare and Galway. The Irish name used today is Cora an Rú, literally translates as the Weir of Rue. Roo is also the name of the adjoining townland in county Galway. Cora comes from the Irish for a weir or ford, which today is acts bridged and marks the Galway/Clare County boundary. The name in historic documents is often referred to as Corra an rúbha. Rúbha is an old Irish and Scottish Gaelic word that refers to a headland or inlet of the sea. There are numerous places with rúbha in the name in the western islands and coast of Scotland (for example Rubha an Dùnain, Rubha Dubh, Rubha na Maighdein. Rubha Mhìcheil) and in Northern Ireland.

Section 3.
Poets and Playwrights

4. The Tale of The O'Dalaigh Poets

Introduction

For the thousands of people who take a walk there every year, the opening lines from the famous poem 'Postscript', will forever associate the Flaggy Shore with the poem's author Seamus Heaney. On a visit, he was enthralled by the wild beauty of the sea, wind, lake, and swans, which served to *"catch the heart off guard and blow it open"*. Yet within a mile of the Flaggy Shore there is a memorial on a hexagonal stone pillar to another great poet, whose obituary in the Annals of the Four Masters for the 13th century stated him to be 'a *poet who was and never will be surpassed'*. A poet who was named, the 'Irish Ovid' because of the richness and smoothness of his verse. That poet was Donnchadh O'Dalaigh who died in 1244.

Donnchadh O'Dalaigh

Donnchadh was the first of a long line of O'Dalaigh poets to settle in Finavarra. Born in Meath, into an ancient Irish tribe, the race of Dalach of Curcu Adaimh (Corcu Adaimh means race of Adam), he came from a family who had served as poets to the kings of Ireland but who were also local chieftains. Aonghus O'Dalaigh of Corcu Adaimh was the common ancestor and he was said to have had six sons, one of whom was Donnchadh. Following the Anglo-Norman invasion, the Norman political and social culture threatened the way of life of the native rulers and more particularly the role and influence of the poets in the courts of the Gaelic chieftains. While the evidence shows that some branches of the O'Dalaighs stayed in Corcu Adaimh in Leinster, other members scattered west. They set up new seats and bardic schools in Sligo, Roscommon, Clare and West Cork, places where the Norman influence was limited, and Gaelic customs remained unchanged.

Donnchadh O'Dalaigh, arrived in Clare or what was then Thomond, sometime in the 1200's, and served as the Ollamh, i.e., poet of high rank, to the O' Loughlin's, the kings, and chieftains of the Burren. There are 30 poems, religious in content, which have survived for 1000 years which are attributed to him. He was regarded as the master of a style of poetry called Dán Díreach, which had complex rules on rhyme, form and structure designed to be chanted.

While it is recorded, that Donnchadh had sons who succeeded him in his hereditary role as Poet in Chief in Finavarra, it is believed that later in life he became a monk and died at the Cistercian monastery at Boyle Abbey. Up until the end of the 19th century an oak tree still stood there, marking his burial place in the grounds of the abbey. In medieval times, it wasn't unusual for learned men or local kings and chieftains to serve their final days in monasteries to ensure their 'ticket to heaven'.

O'Dalaigh Poets of Finavarra

One of Donnchadh's descendants from Finavarra, living in the early 15th century was Cearbhall O'Dalaigh, famous as a composer and harpist. He was described in the Annals of the Four Masters as *'chief composer in Ireland and Ollamh in Corcomroe'*. He is credited as the composer of the song and tune 'Eileen Aroon'. One anecdote from the 18th century states that Handel first heard the air on a visit to Dublin in 1742. He was so impressed that he declared he would willingly give up the all the fame he had acquired for all his musical compositions for the glory of being the composer of the air Eileen Aroon.

One version of the song's origin is that as a young poet and composer, Cearbhall from Finavarra met and fell in love with Eileen Kavanagh, the daughter of a Leinster chieftain, who resided at Palmanly Castle in Carlow. Her family didn't regard Cearbhall as good enough for their beautiful daughter and while he was away, they arranged a match between her and a more suitable suitor. The day before the wedding Cearbhall returned and disguised as a wandering minstrel, he managed to weave his way into the pre wedding banquet with his harp to entertain the wedding party. There he sang the love song he had composed 'Eileen Aroon', in her honour, through which he declared his love, asking his loved one to come away with him. Recognising her lover through the haunting melody, Eileen is said to have eloped with him to Finavarra to the consternation of her family. Another aspect of the song which has ensured its fame is the claim that the words (repeated three times in the original song); *"Cead Mile Failte romhat"* is regarded as the first rendering of the phase 'One hundred thousand welcomes' which has come to represent Ireland's most famous greeting.

Historical documentation and more particularly the Annals reference several other members of the Dalaighs of

Finavarra between the 13th and 17th centuries. While Donnchadh is credited with the founding of the bardic school in Finavarra, under the patronage of the O'Loughlin's and later the O'Brien's, the school appeared to enjoy continued prominence until the 17th century. In a translation of Gerald of Wales's 12th century account of travels to Ireland, Hooker, an Anglican priest explained to Walter Raleigh, *"Britain has its druids and bards, and Ireland has its O'Daly's or Rimers who being very wise men of great credit did deliver their sayings in metre and therefore called poets."*

Druids – Predecessors of The Poets

The position of the poet in the kings' and chieftains' courts has its roots in the pre- Christian era of the learned druids. In their day the druids were regarded as masters of all learning, both natural and supernatural. Among their accomplishments they were astronomers, healers, historians, mathematicians, and philosophers and were trained in law. often combining the role of brehon or adjudicator.

The earliest reference to Finavarra, Fidh Na Beara, the wood of the Brehons was recorded in the Tripartite Life of St Patrick, written before the 10th century, at least two hundred years before history records that the O'Dalaigh poets set foot in Finavarra. This suggests that it was already a place of assemblies, where crowds gathered and where the brehon adjudicated. A stone platform exists on Boireann mountain which was known at various times as the Druids Chair or the O' Dalaigh Chair. It is marked as St Denis's chair in the ordnance survey map of the 1840's, Denis being the Irish for Donnacha, (the first O'Dalaigh poet to settle in Finavarra). Cooke in the Autumnal Rambles of 1842 described it as follows:

"The chair is a platform about seven or eight feet long by four feet wide, apparently carved by nature, in the side of a large rock overlooking a small amphitheatre shaped glen, in which used to assemble in days long gone by the party's litigant, as well as the people who desired to hear the laws propounded. The Brehon when seated here had an extensive view over sea and wild mountain scenery towards the south and west. The chair itself has an aspect looking south, 25 degrees west."

In the BSD the area is referred to as Dearing alias Derreen alias Ballaknavin. Deáring is the corruption of Doire Na Aenach, which literally means oak wood of the assembly or fair. The popular view is that the word 'Druid" is derived from Doire the Irish-Gaelic word for oak tree (often a symbol of knowledge), but also meaning 'wisdom'. Druids were concerned with the natural world and its powers, and considered trees sacred, particularly the oak. The alternative name Ballaknavin, in Irish Baile Na Cnaimhin the place of the small bones, has sacrificial connotations!

Assemblies, often on mountain tops, in the pre-Christian era were presided over by druids. In Christian times, the brehons and poets, took the place of the druids in leading ceremonies and festivities as well as negotiations and administrating the law. Near the glen that Cooke refers to is the site of three caves. Caves have been the sites of druidic death rituals from prehistoric times. The existence of the assembly places, caves, brehon chair and the name Ballaknavin, Baile Na Cnaimhin, (translated as *the place of the small bones*) all mark the area as an important gathering place for rituals in early times.

Position of Poet

Later when Christianity became widespread the poets' schools and bardic colleges across Ireland took on the mantle and became places of secular learning for poets that served at the courts of kings. They came to represent the learned philosophers, the literati, and masters of knowledge often with the role of poet and Brehon/judge combined.

The rights and office of the poet/bard were enshrined in the Brehon laws. They could not be harmed, insulted, or refused hospitality. They were rewarded generously, enjoyed several favours, exemptions, and sanctuary. It was ordained that a common estate should be set apart for the poets where they could give public instruction on the sciences to the men of Ireland. Royal courts would often grant lands to their bards. In theory the poet's lands were held sacrosanct and could not be pillaged during raiding or warfare. While the role of the poet was partially hereditary, the role of chief ollamh, chief among the poets, was originally by royal appointment. In the later medieval period, the other ollamhs came to elect tone of their number to be chief. Much of the poets' work consists of extended genealogies and exaggerated accounts of the deeds of their lords and ancestors. The praise of a skilled poet was valued as it enhanced the social and political prestige of the subject. However, likewise, the satire or insult of a poet was a cause of dread in a society where it could bring shame and humiliation.

The bardic schools, where the poets and learned men trained, were the universities of the time, where men (only) learned by chanting and verse, in a place that served as a retreat from ordinary life. In his work 'The tribes of Ireland' the 19th century historian O Donovan translated the following description of Finavarra – by Aonghus O'Dalaigh from 1617.

> *"The House of O' Dalaigh grew its wealth.*
> *Bestowing without a folly at a white house*
> *It were a sufficiently loud organ to hear his pupils,*
> *Reciting the melodies of the ancient scholars."*

The school in Finavarra was said to have up to 150 scholars in training at one time. In the Annals of 1514, it was mentioned; *"O Daly Teige of Corcomroe 'a professor of poetry who kept a house of general hospitality died in Finavarra and was buried at Corcomroe."'* In another reference to another member of the family, famous for his hospitality, the annals state; *"Donough O'Dalaigh was renowned for his guesthouse as well as his poetry."*

Anglicisation of Ireland

At various intervals from the 13th to the 17th century, the English monarchs used military intervention to try to impose English rules, laws, and customs upon the Irish. As the Irish chieftains continued to resist, the poets and bards (as in Wales) were seen as inciters of Celtic resistance. In 1403 a law was passed in Wales forbidding bards to follow their tradition.

Sir John Stanley, (1350 – 1414) who served as the Irish Lord Lieutenant was the leader of several campaigns to enforce English rule in Ireland and quell any rebellions. He was seen as especially violent towards learned men or poets and clerics and he *"gave no protection or mercy to clergy, laity, or men of science".* After a raid by Stanley on the lands and cows of O'Higgins, a Gaelic chieftain in Meath, the O'Higgins's poet satirized Stanley who coincidentally died in Ardee County Louth in 1414, five weeks later. The poets were jubilant; they had *'berhymed him to death'* using the death dealing power of satirical poetry. His cause of death was said to have been a result of the *'virulence of the lampoons'* implying the power of the poets. Lord Furnivale (1384- 1452), his successor as Lord Lieutenant, arrived in Ireland determined to revenge his predecessor's death. The Annals of Ulster record: *"That from the time of Herod there come no one so wicked"* He is recorded as having dissipated many of the poets of Ireland and it is documented in the Annals of the Four Masters that in 1410, he plundered the Dalaigh's of Meath and of Corcomroe (Finavarra), killing all before him.

There were repeated attempts by English monarchs over the following centuries to rid Ireland of its Gaelic traditions and laws, which was typified by the role, prestige, and influence of the poets. But throughout this period, it would appear from the evidence available that the O'Dalaighs of Finavarra maintained their standing and their name continued to be synonymous with poets and brehons. By the end of the 16th century, they also were now chieftains, possessing large estates, including lands in Parkmore under their own name.

In the 1540s Murrough O'Brien the King of Thomond gave up his native title of King of Thomond and assumed the title of Earl of Thomond and his nephew became the Baron of Inchiquin. The peerages were bestowed on them by Henry VIII and were conditional upon the adoption of Tudor customs and laws. This was part of the Anglicisation of Ireland which continued under Queen Elizabeth I, through what became known as 'surrender and re-grant'. In 1583 the Composition of Connaught extended these agreements between the English Administration and Connaught chieftains, whereby the Gaelic rulers surrendered their lands and received them back with a royal patent. Under the new administration the former chieftains were required to swear allegiance, pay a specified rent to the crown and their overlords, and implement English customs and Common Law. As part of this process, in 1583 the Earl of Thomond entered an agreement with the O'Loughlin and other chieftains in Clare for them to pay annual rent in place of military service and tributes as under the old administration governed by Brehon Law.

The Earls of Thomond set up several manor courts in Clare to enforce English Common Law and so began the progression away from native Brehon Courts. But the evidence shows that the Earl continued to use members of the old poetic and bardic learned families as jury members under the new system. The Inchiquin Manuscripts record that in 1591 a branch of the O'Dalaighs were granted the rich lands of Finavarra by Earl of Thomond for 100 years. The record states; *"The Earl of Thomond, as lord of Sliocht Mela-ghlin, regranted the O'Daly bardic family (Muintir Dála), their holding of 'the four sheisiodh of Finavarra for one hundred years from May 1591 for services due and accustomed in law"*. Their services under the new administration would clearly be different, but it's a reflection that the O'Briens although outwardly anglicized still valued and were influenced by the older Gaelic traditions and the propaganda power of the poet.

The changes implemented from this period were far-reaching and alien to the native traditions and began the social eclipse of the bardic families who depended on Gaelic Chieftains for their patronage. Loughlan Og O'Dalaigh of Finavarra in 1610 wrote a poem lamenting the passing of the native society and culture in Ireland. *"Where have all the Gaels gone, in their place we have a proud impure swarm of foreigners"*. Yet two years later, in 1612 Donough, son of Loughlan Rue O'Dalaigh of Finavarra, sold to Anthony Lynch of Galway his share of the O'Dalaigh estate at Finavarra. In the deed (translated from Irish by Hardiman) he agreed to give in return for payment in English crowns *"half a quarter mire of Gortnadrise of the townland of Finavarra itself with its scite (dung heap), garden and dwelling, pasture, arable land, and water"*. which the family as poets had been given by the O'Briens twenty years earlier. The family continued as landowners, but also as tenants in Finavarra. According to the 1670 census, Teige O'Daly is registered as a gentleman of Finavarra. An incident is recorded in the same year, whereby a wandering musician arrived at the house of O'Dalaigh and following a poem in praise of the owner, the O'Dalaigh took him aside, telling him:

"Friend, I admire your composition, and thank you for the honour you do me. As a reward I will give you some advice — the profession of a bard is now but a precarious means of subsistence, relinquish it, therefore, for a more profitable one. We ourselves pursued the profession only while it was attended with emolument."

Clearly the days when you could make a living as a poet had passed!

The influence of the O'Dalaighs at the ancestral seat at Corca Adaimh in Meath continued until the mid-17th century when it was ransacked and the lands destroyed by the Cromwellian adventurers, one of whom declared, after leaving just one tree standing that its purpose was *"to hang the chief of O'Dalaigh should he ever try to return or endeavour to renew a residence here"*. In his book Tribes of Ireland written in 1850, O'Donovan makes a fitting tribute; *"there is certainly no family to which the bardic literature of Ireland is more deeply indebted from 1139 Cochonoght O'Dalaigh to Carroll Oge O'Daly who lived about 1650"*.

But the O'Dalaighs weren't just poets, after the demise of the bardic traditions, many who had been educated in the bardic schools became priests and monks. In this period, after the dissolution of the monasteries Catholic priests and friars were outlawed. Frost in his history of County Clare tells that in 1579, Teige O' Daly of Finavarra, a friar of the order of Saint Frances, was arrested in the Franciscan Convent at Askeaton and executed.

Remains of The Bardic School and Guest House of O'Dalaighs

A stone building, which was reputed to be the remains of the bardic school, was still visible in Finavarra demesne up until the middle of the 19th century. Today the southwest corner of the walled garden in the demesne, facing the sea, incorporates one of the gable walls, the only remaining part of the stone building.

In his visits to New Quay in the late 1830s and early 1840's T.L. Cooke (Author of Autumnal Rambles around New Quay) stayed at Leatha Lodge in Parkmore. Close by the former site of Leatha Lodge, there are some ruins which Cooke described.

> *"In the field close by Daly's monument are the ruins of some extensive building which tradition says was once a school. Here also yet remains an excavation in a large rock, resembling a huge Apothecary's mortar. It was probably used for bruising corn (it more probably was one of those Rock-basins coevals (contemporary) with paganism in Ireland). There is likewise an underground cave, seemingly of the mithric kind in the same field."*

The site, (although with scant remains today, nearly two hundred years after Cooke's visit), is referred to locally as the Monks House and the *ruins of the extensive buildings* may have been the remains of the guest house and the home of the brehon. In the 17th century will of James Fitzmaurice Skerrett, he refers to the estate he purchased at Tinavarra and several other Skerrett estate 19th century documents reference their lands at Tinavarra. Tinavarra is the anglicisation of Tigh Na Bheara, translated as the House of the Judge or Brehon. So, is the monk referred to in the "Monks House" Donnchadh O'Dalaigh, the first O'Dalaigh in Finavarra who in later life became a Cistercian Monk at the abbey in Boyle?

The 1824 survey of schools in Ireland cites the existence of a hedge school at Tinavarra in the parish of Oughtmama. The school, by 1824, after the ending of the penal laws was legally run. It was described as a miserable hovel, and had 65 pupils, 64 Catholics and one Protestant. The headmaster was Thomas Scanlon, and he received an annual income of approximately 26 shillings. When bardic schools were outlawed in the 17th century, many of the teachers and pupils adapted to teach illegally in hedge schools, where teaching the classics alongside Gaelic culture, reading, writing and arithmetic became commonplace. Running a hedge school in the vicinity of what was once a famous bardic school and the home of the bards and brehons of old was deeply symbolic during the time of the penal laws when Gaelic traditions and religion were suppressed. In 1831 a new education system was adopted in Ireland. Schools were paid for by the state and all schools were required to teach the same subjects. Teaching through the medium of Irish or lessons in the Irish language were not allowed. The 1842 ordnance survey maps show a School House near New Quay harbour. This school would have replaced the fee-paying hedge schools in Tinavarra and one in the Catholic chapel at Dooneen. In 1858, Colonel White, the local landlord (who purchased the estates previously owned by the Scott family and those of Burton Bindon in the 1850's), gave a site for a new school beside the lake at Ballyvelaghan. The *Munster News* on the 9th of October 1858, published the following: *"Wanted tenders for a National School and offices in New Quay County Clare to accommodate 150 children. Plans can be viewed at the offices of William Lane Joynt."* Three years later the same newspaper announced that the school was ready to be opened, publishing: *"A National School is about to be opened at New Quay by liberality of Colonel White's representative Alderman Joynt, of Limerick, who as land agent is the consistent friend of education."*

O'Dalaigh Monument

Today a monument, or Leacht, to the memory of Donnchadh O'Dalaigh can be seen on top of a mound close by Pouldoody Bay at Parkmore. The inscription on the pillar is like others found on other *Cuimhne Leachts*, which were quite common in Galway on roadsides as commemoration of people from the late 17th and early 18th century. These stone memorials were built during the time of the penal laws and Catholic churches were either demolished or closed, so in their places, the Catholic gentry used wayside monuments to commemorate the dead. While the dedication to Donnchadh O'Dalaigh, may be from the 17th/18th century, the history of the mound is more far reaching. The use of mounds as places of gatherings goes back to the first centuries of the first millennium. In Gaelic Ireland mounds were common meeting places, used for inauguration and other ceremonies, where the chieftain or bard stood on the top, the mounds beneath were often burial chambers dating to the pre-Christian era. The site, many of which were used as places of ritual by druids were chosen to provide a link with the ancestors buried beneath. Although it hasn't been excavated it's a local belief that the mound close by Pouldoody holds the bones of the dead. With the passing of the Gaelic customs and the central role played by the bard, in the 17th century the site continued to be used as a place of exchange. The pillar has the hallmarks of a market cross but also served as a marker for boats in the bay, to direct them to Parkmore Quay where wool and raw linen was gathered for export.

The legacy of the Dalaigh's learned tradition in New Quay was lasting and, in their footsteps, came others, centuries later; W.B. Yeats, Seamus Heaney and the poet philosopher John O'Donohue.

10. Remains of the O'Dalaigh bardic school in the Finavarra Demesne

11. The O'Dalaigh Monument at Parkmore which includes an inscription on a plaque dedicated to the memory of the 'venerable poet', Donnchadh Mór Ó Dálaigh

5. The Tale of Mount Vernon Lodge

Origins of Mount Vernon Lodge

In 1912 when Lady Gregory purchased Mount Vernon Lodge on the Flaggy Shore as a present for her son William Robert Gregory, she was rekindling a family association with the house which had started with her great grandfather Colonel William Persse. He is reputed to have built the house near the seashore in the 1780s. The Georgian villa, painted white with red windows, is a distinctive landmark on the Flaggy Shore. The house faces north towards Galway Bay and the cliffs of Aughnish while the original walled garden and outbuildings are still in existence. A field lies to the front, which until recently contained a pond, fed from the sea water under the road. It is thought that at an earlier period this was designed to hold fresh young oysters imported from Connemara, situated as it was next to the old pier.

The Persse family had their seat at Roxborough House near Loughrea in County Galway. At its peak in the 19th century the Persse estate consisted of nearly 12,000 acres in Galway, Roscommon, and Clare. The family belonged to the

Anglo-Irish Protestant ascendancy and were dominant in the political, economic, and social life of Connaught up until the early twentieth century. Colonel William Persse (1728 – 1803) inherited Roxborough in the mid 18th century. He was instrumental in setting up the Irish Volunteer Force. The Volunteer force was created with the primary aim of resisting an invasion from France or Spain during the American War of Independence. He created the first branch of the volunteers outside Dublin in Roxborough in 1777. He personally trained and armed a group of sixty men, dressing them in the uniform of scarlet, with blue facings while awarding himself the title of colonel. He was also a strong advocate of trade reform and used the bargaining power of the volunteers to try to get concessions from the British for Irish trade particularly in wool. He took many of his liberal views and the inspiration for taking on the establishment from George Washington, his friend and correspondent. His admiration led him to name his property on the Flaggy Shore 'Mount Vernon' (the name of George Washington's home) in his honour.

The story of how George Washington (the first president of the United States)'s home came to be known as Mount Vernon is an interesting one. Washington's father Augustine brought his family to live at Little Hunting Creek plantation in Virginia in 1734. The plantation, consisting of 3,000 acres, was left to George's brother Lawrence in 1743 on his father's death. Lawrence, who had been a soldier in the English army, renamed the estate Mount Vernon in honour of Admiral Edward Vernon. Vernon was the British commander of the Virginia Foot Regiments in which Lawrence had served. It's ironic that Vernon represented British imperialism and British colonial power, colonialism that George Washington successfully fought when he gained American independence. However, George retained the name of the plantation when he inherited the estate, having leased it for many years from his brother's widow. In later years Washington devoted much of his time developing the gardens, plants, and fruit trees at Mount Vernon.

Correspondence between Persse, his close friend Edward Newnham and Washington began with political empathy and support for the achievement of American Independence, but in later years centred around gardening and a shared love for horticulture. Much of the correspondence has been lost but what remains provides evidence that Persse had sent gooseberry bushes and hay seeds to George Washington with instructions for planting. He also tried to send as a gift a pack of Irish Wolf hounds, but the logistics of transporting them to America proved too difficult. Washington reciprocated with his own gifts. The three large Pine trees, which today dominate the skyline at the back of Mount Vernon on the Flaggy Shore, are reputed to have been a gift from George Washington. Lady Gregory also told of a gift of a glass case of stuffed birds, that had been on display in Roxborough, her childhood home.

When Colonel William Persse's first wife Sarah Blakeney died in the 1780s, he married Sarah Persse, daughter of Francis Persse (his cousin) and Sarah Skerrett. Sarah, his new mother- in- law was first cousin to Hyacinth Skerrett of Finavarra. It may have been through the Skerrett connection that William Persse first came to purchase land in Ballyconneen, the Flaggy Shore townland. The Parliamentary archives show that in 1787 William Persse and Hyacinth Skerrett together petitioned parliament to provide additional funding for a pier they had built with private funds at Blenview in the Burren in County Clare.

1800 - 1880

Records show that the Persse family continued to have property in the parish of Oughtmama in County Clare until the middle of the 19th century. In the 1829 tithe records, John Hynes is recorded as living in Mount Vernon. However, this may have been a short-term rent, as the freeholders lists for county Clare for 1821 and 1829 include the Persse's as the landowners of the townland of Ballyconneen. The 1845 Valuation Office includes Dudley Persse as a household owner in New Quay. However, by the time of the Griffith's Valuation, 1856, Mount Vernon was owned by the Skerrett family and leased to Captain Bagot.

From the early 19th century, the Flaggy Shore was a popular summer destination for the gentry from Clare, Gort and east Galway. The Victorians believed in the medicinal powers of bathing in the sea and breathing in the sea air, so just as they enjoyed winters abroad and seasons in London or Dublin, visits to the Flaggy Shore in the summer season became part of the annual ritual for the West of Ireland Anglo-Irish gentry. In his biography, Valentine William, (grandson of William Skerrett) describes the gathering of the Ascendancy at the Flaggy Shore for bathing and socialising. The Skerretts owned many of the lodges around the Flaggy Shore and in the Summer rented them to visitors and their gentry friends. The Galway Vindicator archives contain numerous advertisements advertising these houses for rent, including Villa Marina, Mount Vernon, and the Beach House, all of which could be rented for a month, a summer or for longer. The arrival of these visitors was mentioned in the society columns, for instance in 1873 the Galway Vindicator reported that the following had arrived in the Flaggy Shore for the Summer season; the Seymours from Somerset (East Galway) staying at Mount Vernon, the Persse family and Shaw Taylors (family of Eliza Persse) staying at Cartron House and the Cowans (family of Helen Skerrett) staying at Stormy Hall.

From the 1860's a steamer sailed between Ballyvaughan, Kinvara and Galway bringing visitors from Galway to the

Burren. However, to the consternation of William Skerrett, the owners of the steamer refused to dock in New Quay because of the poor state of the pier and dependence on the tide times. Alongside Captain Bagot, William Skerrett tried to secure Government funding for a new pier in the 1870s but without success. Skerrett provided a plot of land for a protestant chapel beside the shore where Church of Ireland weekly services were held during the summer season. This catered for the large number of protestant families holidaying close by. The chapel was dismantled in 1961 and the ornate gates moved to the old gate lodge for Finavarra House, where they can still be seen.

For the local people, the arrival of the gentry in their carriages and fine clothes must have bought some opportunities for paid employment as domestic servants, but their day-to-day toil to make a living from the land or sea would not have changed substantially. The contrast between the local people and the land-owning class is evidenced by one instance in 1855 in which the Rev. Jackson, the vicar who lived at New Quay House, took a local farmer to court for allowing his ass to graze on the church grounds. The farmer was fined a shilling.

1880 – 1930s

As a child Lady Gregory, would have been a frequent summer visitor to the Flaggy Shore along with her siblings and parents from Roxborough. In 1880, Lady Gregory, then known as Isabella Augusta Persse, 5th daughter of Dudley and Frances Persse, married Sir William Gregory a widower and thirty-five years her senior. A year later in 1881 Lady Gregory gave birth to their only son William Robert Gregory. Until Sir William's death in 1892, the couple travelled extensively abroad and kept a house in London with occasional visits back to Coole. Lady Gregory's role in the Irish

Literary Revival and the founding of the Abbey Theatre with W.B. Yeats and Edward Martyn is well documented. Her home in Coole Park became the centre where artists, writers, playwrights, and poets gathered and became the focal point for those who shaped the literary revival. Her gradual awakening interest in Celtic folklore, legends, myths, and superstitions of the local people began in the 1890s. She wrote:

> *"I was becoming conscious of a world close to me that I had been ignorant of up until now. It was not now in the corners of newspapers I looked for poetic emotion, not even to the sayers of the street. It was among farmers, potato diggers and old men in workhouses and beggars at my own door that I found what was beyond and yet further than the drawing room part of my childhood, in the expression of love and grief and the pain of parting, that are the disclosures of the individual soul."* (Kiltartan Book P20)

In 1897 she rented Harbour Hill House (which later became the local constabulary) in New Quay for a month during which she spent her time collecting stories of fairies, forts, banshees, and ghosts. She wrote an article for the Spectator called "Irish Visions" while she was in New Quay. In it she spoke of her amazement and the revelation that the country people she had lived among for 45 years, inhabited a world of belief of which she had very little awareness. Her imagination was caught by the fact that in the Burren landscape the lives of the people, their beliefs, and the words they used to describe their beliefs and experiences, seemed to be one of a piece. She wrote of the perception that folklore was an intrinsic part of their lives, as natural as the landscape and an inevitable result of its airy blueness; *"Shadows of cloud and rock by day and shadows of thoughts of dreams of the dead by night"*. Valentine Williams ascribes the source of many of the stories, to Martin Minogue, a local one-eyed fisherman from New Quay, whose poetic turn of phrase and exaggerations in the telling of the stories of siaidhes, ghosts and ring forts, had Lady Gregory enthralled.

In the same year 1897 that Lady Gregory stayed at Harbour Hill House, WB Yeats, also visited New Quay for the first time. While staying with Edward Martyn at Doorus he took the poet Arthur Symons with him to the Burren. Like Gregory, they were captivated by the local stories of the supernatural. In 1897 Symons wrote the poem: 'In the Wood of Finavarra':

"I have grown tired of sorrow and human tears;
Life is a dream in the night, a fear among fears,
A naked runner lost in a storm of spears.
I have grown tired of rapture and love's desire;
Love is a flaming heart, and its flames aspire
Till they cloud the soul in the smoke of a windy fire.

I would wash the dust of the world in a soft green flood;
Here between sea and sea, in the fairy wood,
I have found a delicate, wave-green solitude.

Here, in the fairy wood, between sea and sea,
I have heard the song of a fairy bird in a tree,
And the peace that is not in the world has flown to me."

In the 1970s people still remembered Lady Gregory's frequent visits to New Quay. She was remembered as a warm-hearted friendly woman, generous and kind, in contrast to Yeats who always came across as an awkward, sullen character never at ease with ordinary people. In the early 20th century, she sought a more permanent base in New Quay when she purchased a holiday home for her family.

In 1912 Helena Skerrett put Mount Vernon Lodge up for sale. The following particulars are taken from the *Evening Irish Times* on Saturday 03 August 1912.

"SALE - MOUNT VERNON. NEW QUAY CO. CLARE. VALUABLE HOUSEHOLD PROPERTY. TO BE SOLD BY PUBLIC AUCTION. ON TUES-DAY. 6th August 1912.

At the hour of One o Clock on the grounds. The Subscriber has been favoured with instruction from Mrs Skerrett to sell by public auction the above valuable property. The house, which is beautifully situated facing Galway, standing in its own grounds about 3 acres (statute) is a two-story building containing drawing room, dining room, five bedrooms, kitchen, scullery, pantries etc.

There are also substantial out-offices, stabling, coach houses, etc and a large garden surrounded by a high wall all situated within a few minutes of post and telegraph offices. The house lets during the summer months from £13 to £15 per month. The property will be sold free of rent for ever. and the rates and taxes are nominal. There Is good fishing and shooting in the neighbourhood. The valuable health-giving qualities of New Quay and its popularity as a summer resort are well known. The Auctioneer begs to draw the attention of intending purchasers to this valuable property as a sound and safe investment.

Terms of Sale. Offers will be received and considered up to the day before Sale.

For further particulars and permission to view apply to: W. M. MITCHELL AUCTIONEERS AND VALUERS GORT."

In 1907 Lady Gregory's only child and heir (William) Robert married Margaret Parry a fellow artist who he had met at the Slade Art School in London. Lady Gregory bought Mount Vernon in 1912 and presented it as a gift to her son and his wife. In their early years of marriage Lady Gregory encouraged the couple to travel abroad and paint while she continued to manage matters at Coole and looked after their children. The couple spent time living in Paris and Italy returning for summers to Coole and the Flaggy Shore.

Their friends were a London bohemian artist group, dominated by the painter Augustus John. Augustus John served as a mentor to Robert Gregory and was best man at his wedding, so when a portrait of Yeats was required for the cover of his new book of poetry, a bulletin edition, Robert persuaded his mother that Augustus John was the best person to do it. Always short of cash, Augustus was enticed to come to Coole, by the offer of £18 and the opportunity to complete some other portraits while there.

In subsequent letters Yeats described Augustus John's arrival: *"this flamboyant youth in a blue jersey and earrings and carrying all his luggage on the end of one finger"*. The finished portrait horrified Lady Gregory, her impression was he had depicted Yeats as an ugly ruffian. Yeats described it thus: *"If one looked like any of the pictures the country women of Kiltartan would run to take the clean clothes off the hedges when one passed as they do at the sight of a tinker"*. Yeats later came round to liking the picture and in 1933 he sent it to a publisher requesting it to be on the cover of his Collection of Poetry. Although from John's perspective the visit may not have been as profitable as he had hoped, it served as his first introduction to the west of Ireland.

Through his friendship with Frances McNamara, Augustus John was to pay numerous visits in subsequent years, to Doolin, (the home of Frances McNamara) and the west of Ireland. The Burren including New Quay, Galway and Connemara were to prove rich territory for him as a painter. Just as Lady Gregory held open house at Coole, Robert and Margaret invited their friends to Mount Vernon and the Flaggy Shore. The fireplaces at Mount Vernon are said to be designed by Augustus John during one of his visits.

The Gregorys, Robert and Margaret appear to have been happily married for seven years, when the artists Nora and Gerald Summers came into their lives. The Summers were invited to Coole in 1915 and then rented a bungalow at the

Flaggy Shore. During the summer at Mount Vernon, Margaret became aware than Robert was having an affair with 23-year-old Nora Summers. When Robert refused to end the affair and made no secret of his obsession, Margaret was devastated. Tired of the endless rows, Robert made the decision to enlist in the air force. While he had considered enlisting at the beginning of World War 1, events at Coole, with tenants and the Land Commission clamouring for sale of the Gregory estate, his mother persuaded him he was needed at home. However, as difficulties within his marriage intensified, he signed up and joined the war effort. During the short time as a fighter pilot from 1915 with the Royal Flying Corps, he excelled much more than he had ever as an artist and painter. He proved himself a brave combat fighter, receiving medals for his bravery including the Military Cross for 'conspicuous gallantry and devotion to duty'. Six months after joining, George Bernard Shaw (GBH) met him in Paris. GBH was able to report to Lady Gregory that Robert, although recovering from a severe bout of frostbite on his face, was in excellent spirits and had declared that the six months flying had been the happiest time of his life! On temporary leave in London, Robert and Margaret became reconciled but soon after, Robert's plane crashed over Padua and he was killed, age 36 in the year 1917. The news of his death came as a devastating blow to both Margaret and his mother. The story of his life and death was immortalised by Yeats in the poem "An Irish Airman foresees his death".

As well as the death of her only son, Lady Gregory had also been distraught on hearing of the drowning of her favourite nephew and protégé Hugh Lane. Hugh Lane was a passenger on the Lusitania when it sank off the south coast in May 1915. When Lady Gregory's sister Adelaide received a marriage proposal from the divinity student James Lane, her parents were reluctant to accept him, on the grounds he was a poor churchman with little prospect. The couple went on to have five children, the youngest of whom was Hugh. Adelaide found it hard to adjust to being poor and living in a rectory in Cornwall, while James was resentful that she didn't bring more of the Persse family's wealth to the marriage. Lady Gregory was instrumental in helping Hugh get an apprenticeship as an art restorer in London. Hugh proved to have a unique eye for talented painters and went on to have a successful career as an art collector, a career that eventually bought him immense wealth and prestige. According to her biography, Lady Gregory apparently got a glimpse of his artistic flair when she caught him modelling her dresses with various accessories. When his parent's marriage broke down, Adelaide, Hugh's mother, risked being left with nothing until Lady Gregory intervened. Lady Gregory tracked down a woman with whom James Lane was romantically linked and got hold of some love letters. Under threat of exposure, he finally agreed to return Adelaide her original marriage dowry of £2000.

Hugh Lane had established Dublin's Municipal Gallery of Modern Art in 1908 for the display of paintings including many by the Impressionist artists which he had acquired. Frustrated by Dublin Corporation's reluctance to fund a more permanent home, he wrote his will leaving the paintings to the National Gallery in London. The dispute over the building of a suitable gallery in Dublin was still on-going when he drowned. Yeats and Lady Gregory, having been in contact with him prior to his death, were both convinced that he had written another will reversing the position. In an effort to find the lost will, Yeats consulted occultists and spiritualists. Lady Gregory, always concerned for Yeats's welfare and in an effort at matchmaking, invited Alick Schepeter to Coole. Yeats seemed attracted to Alick, the former muse of Augustus John. Lady Gregory encouraged the relationship and persuaded her daughter-in-law Margaret to take both to Mount Vernon at New Quay. Alick counted clairvoyancy among her talents, and it turned out that it was this aspect that most interested Yeats. Yeats used Alick to try and put him in touch with Hugh Lane's spirit to find the missing will. Being the practical woman that she was, Lady Gregory decided to take the matter into her own hands, and she ordered a search of Hugh Lane's office in the gallery in Harcourt Street. The codicil to the will was found in a desk drawer. Although signed three times, it had not been witnessed. So started a long-drawn-out dispute between the English and Irish authorities on the validity of the codicil. The dispute was only solved in 1959 when both governments agreed to share and rotate the paintings between the two countries. The efforts to get the paintings for Ireland were driven in no small part by Lady Gregory from 1917 until her death in 1932.

In 1917 Yeats married Georgie Hyde Lees and purchased Thoor Ballylee as his family home. Robert's widow, Margaret Gregory developed a friendship with her Coole neighbour, Guy Gough of Lough Cutra Castle, and she eventually married him in 1928. Richard, Ann and Catherine, the children of Robert and Margaret Gregory continued to spend a lot of their childhood at Coole and at Mount Vernon with their beloved grandmother. In their book about growing up at Coole, Ann and Catherine include memories of times at Mount Vernon, fishing by the Flaggy Shore, watching Mike Minogue gallop his horse across the strand and helping at the threshing at Tierney's where they were allowed to lead the horse. Anne recalls being allowed, to the consternation of Lady Gregory's driver, to drive the car from Coole to Clare aged thirteen!

On the 22nd of May 1932 Lady Gregory, who had been allowed to stay on in Coole Park for her lifetime, died. Four years later Margaret sold Mount Vernon. While the Gregory family home at Coole Park has been demolished, Mount Vernon still stands as a relic to a vanished past, a relic of the class system but more famously as a testament to the indomitable spirit of one woman, Lady Gregory and her contribution to the literary revival and arts in Ireland.

12. Contemporary view of Mount Vernon Lodge

Section 4.
Sea Trade, Fishing and The Oyster Baron

6. The Tale of Sea Trade and Fishing

Lough Lurgan

According to Roderic O'Flaherty writing in the 1680's, Galway Bay was once a giant lake, one of the three largest in Ireland. Repeating tales from ancient sources, he wrote of a time when a tsunami of water engulfed the west of Ireland and the Atlantic Ocean broke through, flooding the lake with sea water. According to his sources, the three islands of Arran are all that remains of that outer bank.

> *"Lough Lurgan is a spacious inlet of the sea, between Thomond and West Connaught at the mouth of Galway and extending at a great distance to the east, which formerly was separated perhaps by strong banks, until the Western Ocean undermining the confines of the sea, united with itself. The remains of the banks appear to be the three islands of Aran."*

The historical accuracy of O Flaherty's description is questionable. However, research by the late NUIG geologist Professor Mike Waters did find evidence of 7500 years old drowned forests beneath the sea along the north side of

Galway Bay. He deduced that Galway Bay may once have been wetlands and that over time, with the advancing tide and climate change, trees became submerged beneath bogs and the water levels of the Atlantic rose and spread inland.

In the 1840's TL Cooke wrote in his *Autumnal Rambles around New Quay*:

> *"It is said that the remains of an ancient wood, consisting of oak trees laid side-long, and without leaves or branches, has been discovered in the sea under low water mark, about half-way between the Flaggy shore and Finavarra point."*

The existence of these trees preserved beneath the sea is also backed up by local folklore. However, no evidence has been uncovered to determine if the trees are the remains of ancient woodlands, from islands that have got submerged with rising seas levels, ancient trackways, or even medieval fish traps.

Sea Trade

Galway Bay has for centuries been important as a thoroughfare for trade along the western seaboard stretching to Spain, Portugal, France, and Scotland. In the absence of roadways, the sea provided the main route for trade and travel, and this continued to be the case until the development of roads and railways in the mid 19th century. A survey in 2008, identified several small quays, jetties, and piers along the Clare coast, many predating the 19th century. The list included: two landing places at Currenrue, two at Munnia, an older, as well as the current quay at New Quay, Skerretts Quay and Parkmore in Finavarra, Bellharbour and Aughinish. Even before the harbour at New Quay was built in the 1820's these smaller landing places were used for small scale local fishing in shallow waters and by fishermen involved in oyster, mussels, crab, and lobster fishing as well as seaweed harvesting.

But these landing places also had a role to play in transport and trade along the Atlantic coast.

Lynches – Maritime Activities

During the 15th, 16th. and early 17th century the Galway merchants built up considerable foreign trade on which the wealth of the city was founded. The Lynches were one of the leading merchant families, which flourished first from within the city walls but later, by the end of the 16th century, they began to use their wealth to expand outside the city. The Composition of Connaught in 1582, was a major turning point for Gaelic rule within Connaught and County Clare. It resulted in much of the Gaelic systems with authority vested in local chiefs being swept away and increased anglicisation and commercialisation of land ownership. No longer controlled by the constraints of traditional Brehon and hereditary rules, many of the Gaelic chieftains were happy to sell their lands and leases and this afforded the Galway merchants the opportunity to invest their surplus incomes in purchasing landed estates in Galway, Mayo, and Clare. The Lynches owed much of their success to their mastery of the sea, and their skills as sailors, traders, and adventurers.

The 1641 list of leaseholders for each townland in the Burren (compiled in the 1656 Down Survey), shows that the Lynches were the primary landowners for much of the coastal land in present day New Quay, Ballyvaughan and Fanore. Martin Lynch had leases of lands and was the principal landowner in Finavarra and in Munnia as well as in Lisnanard and Gurtahallaha townlands in Drumcreehy Parish. James Lynch had lands in the townland of Lisconera (sea inlets) in Killonagh Parish and in Murough in the parish of Gleninagh Parish. Dominick Lynch was the principal landowner at Dangan in Drumcreehy Parish. The Lynches bought up most of the arable land and while farming was important, the vicinity of the land to the coast facilitated their access to trade by the sea.

From the 1590's St Malo in France was the principal destination for much of the trade from Galway. The Lynches had the advantage of having family connections in both towns. Their lands on the coast gave the Lynches access to jetties where small boats used to ferry goods out to the ships anchored in Galway Bay. The O'Dalaigh monument which stands in Parkmore, served as a Market Cross. Although it is in better condition, its design is almost identical with the Bandle Cross which stands next to Nougheval church. Both would have marked a site for market exchange. The word bandle has a couple of meanings, one is a unit of measurement of approximately two metres, but in Ireland it was also an old word for homespun linen. In 1745 Arthur Young in his Tour of Ireland describes *"Bandle, or narrow linen, for home consumption, is made in the western part of the county"*. The structure of the Nougheval Cross was possibly used as a measure of the width of the fabric traded. The location of the Finavarra stone pillar was a marker for boats to guide them to the small landing place at Parkmore, where wool and linen, spun in local houses, and other agricultural produce were exchanged for export. Parkmore, like many of the small piers around Galway Bay would only have been accessible from the sea at high tide and even then, only small boats such as curraches would have been able to land. The goods were brought from the interior and exchanged at the jetty where they were transported out to larger boats and ships in the bay for export for France.

Cromwellian Wars and The Penal Laws

In 1671, following the Cromwellian wars and the restoration of the monarchy, the Lynches' name had disappeared from the list of landowners of North Clare. The land within a mile of the coast was reserved for the soldiers and adventurers who fought on the side of the English, many of whom received lands instead of payment for their services. With the banishment of the Galway tribes from the town, Galway also ceased to be as important or prosperous and, trade with France and Spain dwindled.

New legislation implemented by the British government in the 1720s prohibited Irish merchants from selling wool abroad anywhere except England. The strong demand in France for Irish wool, led to an active trade in smuggling around Galway Bay. Research by the historian Louis Cullen into the trade with France showed evidence of foreign ships sailing from Galway to Nantes bringing wool and returning with French produce, including tea and tobacco. The boats sailed from Galway harbour with their legitimate cargo, stopping in Roundstone Harbour. Smaller boats circled the bay and wool purchased locally was taken to Roundstone where it was loaded onto the bigger ships for Nantes. To prevent smuggling, the authorities kept a ship called *HMS Spy* in Galway Bay, but evidence shows that smuggling was rife, involving not just the leading landowners (among them families of the former Galway tribes, the Kerwins and Blakes) but also those placed in charge to collect the taxes. Louis Cullen uncovered a cache of letters which includes the excerpt below.

> *"James Disney, the Collector's son, and James Figgi, the Barrack-master of this town, runs as much wool as any of the gang, which the said James Disney and James Figgi holds a farm in the county of Clare [which] is called Aughinish and gathers all their wool there and send it from that place to Connemara and ships it off at Round Stone Bay."*

Deeds from the early 18th century show James Disney as renting land in Aughinish from the Bishop of Killaloe, so besides being the son of the His Majesty's Tax Collector for the port of Galway, he was also the ringleader in wool smuggling.

Fishing

The riches afforded by the sea extended beyond opportunities for trade, legitimate or otherwise. In the 18th century the seas around Galway Bay teemed with fish, but for places like New Quay there were limited opportunities for fishing. The harbours or landing places were not deep enough for large boats to dock and there was no means of preserving any fish that could be landed. All along the Scottish seaboard from the Northern Isles the fishing industry flourished as the British Fishing Society from the 1780's developed ports and facilities where legions of women were employed in gutting and salting fish. Hyacinth Skerrett of Finavarra and William Persse of Roxborough sought to get funding to develop similar in North Clare.

According to their petition in 1787 to the Irish parliament, Skerrett and Persse had built a quay in the Burren with their own funds. They wanted a harbour which was more easily accessible and not dependent on the ebb and flow of the tide. Wishing to exploit the fishing opportunities, their petition requested Government funding to develop the harbour and buildings for salting fish and accommodation of people involved in the industry as well as coopers to build the fish cages. The petition in March 1787 (from the Irish Parliamentary Journals) stated: *"That great shoals of herrings, cod and ling annually resort to the shores of County Clare on the western shore of this kingdom and where a great number of vessels annually assemble for the purpose of fishing."* However, the benefits of this rich source of fish were lost; *"From the want of a proper or sufficient number of houses to receive all persons concerned in said fishery or a proper establishment of refineries of salt or shores to deposit foreign salt or buildings to cure the fish and coopers to prepare the cases, the opportunities of very considerable national advantage are lost."* They stated in their petition that they, Skerrett and Persse, the petitioners, had already spent their own money building a quay that afforded shelter from the strong winds and had built seaworthy boats for fishing. However, to take full advantage, they were requesting parliament to approve the expenditure of £400 a year which they would match by mortgaging their estates.

The new quay that they referred to was probably a quay, close by the current quay at New Quay. An older quay did exist in front of Mount Vernon, but all traces of this quay were demolished when the road at the Flaggy Shore was built, but it appears to have been out of use long before then. The area around Mount Vernon was known and documented as Cuan (meaning harbour) in deeds from the early 1700s, which indicates that a quay already existed here.

There is no evidence that their petition for funding was successful. In fact, in later years, 1792 to 1810, while England was at war with France, the government actively discouraged any pier building or quay development which would have facilitated a French invasion. In 1806, Parliament passed a decree that no pier could be developed in Ireland without first notifying and getting approval from the Admiralty.

The situation changed in the late 1810's when it became in British interests to develop the Irish fisheries industry. The Commission for fisheries was set up in 1819 for the promotion of fishing in Ireland. One of the first acts was the funded bounty scheme to finance the fitting out of ships. This act stipulated that the owners of fishing vessels involved in herring fishing would be given an allowance for catching and curing herrings, provided they adhered to rules relating to quantities of fish and salt on board. Whilst the funding only benefited owners of large ships, it also meant that smaller boats could be used by local fishermen to catch fish and sell on to the larger boat owners.

Recognizing opportunities, Peter Comyn, a local magistrate, landlord and the owner of a salt house in Murtyclough, pleaded for the construction of a new harbour in the parish. The salt house (at the T junction between the lakes) was used as a place for salting fish and meat for preservation. In his letter to the Irish Fisheries in 1820 he stated:

> *"It cannot have escaped your intelligent mind, what a great benefit would be derived to the properties and inhabitants in the neighbourhood reside in, if a good and safe harbour were made in the stream of the Burrin, when small, decked vessels, good draft could come in at low water."*

In his letter he referred to previous plans to build a pier further out, but which had to contend with the elements. He also referred to the futility of current plans underway, under which

> *"The capital now employed in building small, decked stoops or cutters, fit to stand in the bay in all weathers, and take fish, will cost a good sum."*

His proposals also suggested that the Government which had granted the Fishing Company of Connemara permission to import salt tax free should also be extended to his own district for the promotion of fish preservation. He concluded his letter by outlining the practicalities for getting the harbour built.

> *"To obtain the means for a small harbour, fifty yards long and twenty yards broad, communicable by a narrow passage to the stream of Burrin. the landed proprietor must play a liberal part. He must grant the land for such, with room for a quay round eighty feet wide, at a pepper corn rent for ever. The landholders adjoining will also contribute, and the whole neighbouring population will each give a certain number of days, work gratis, to entitle them to the*

freedom of the quay forever, for, if it is not free harbour and quay, it will not succeed."

The landlord he referred to was Bindon Scott who was the landlord for Ballyvelaghan in the 1820s. The Burren Stream that Comyn refers to is most likely to be the site of the current harbour at New Quay opposite Aughinish.

An Engineer Named Nimmo

While Comyn's request for funding was not successful, work was begun on a new quay within a couple of years of his letter. The development of the pier in New Quay and the development of over 22 more in and around Galway Bay between 1822 and 1829 can be attributed in large part to the work of one man, a Scottish engineer called Nimmo. Exceptional rain in the winter of 1821 and spring of 1822 contributed to the failure of the potato crop which resulted in acute food shortages, leaving the poor starving and destitute, particularly in Connaught, Clare, and South Munster. The British government's solution for the alleviation of these extreme circumstances was to provide funding for employment to be distributed through public works.

Alexander Nimmo was appointed as the chief engineer and supervisor of the public works that came under the Commission of Fisheries. Nimmo's remit was to expend the money for the provision of employment through the development of much needed piers and quays which would support the development of the fishing industry but also improve communication and trade. Before any town or parish could get funding to build a pier, it had to be shown that it was for a place where boats could reside in shelter and have sufficient depth of water to allow boats to come and go at all phases of the tide. Piers or quays were to be extended below water or spring tide to be accessible even at the lowest tide.

New Quay was the site for one of the first 23 harbours selected by Nimmo in Galway Bay for development and the only one in North Clare. A request by Burton Bindon for a quay at nearby Currenrue was turned down as the proposed site didn't meet the criteria for accessibility in low tide. Nimmo designed the quay at 'New Quay' and work began in 1822. He chose the site next to two earlier quays. According to Nimmo both quays were already in ruins when work started, and the place was already known as "New Quay" based on the earlier quay to the west of the current quay. This may have been the quay referred to by Skerrett and Persse in their requests for funding from 1789. The site chosen was selected as it had sufficient depth of water and according to Nimmo *"a good place to run for from easterly winds"*. Nimmo made the following report to the Fisheries Commission in 1825:

"Within Aughnish Bay an inlet runs up four miles to Currenrue bridge and tide mill; the mouth is narrow, about two hundred yards wide; the interior lagoon has some good oyster-beds. The tide ebbs at the entrance of this inlet with considerable force, forming a channel of two and a-half fathoms deep, but without is a bar of nine feet only; the upper part of the inlet is shallow. This is a favourite bathing-place, and there is a considerable population, especially in summer. At the entrance of the inlet, on the south side, two attempts have been made to build a quay, the village was also named New Quay; but both are in ruins. Indeed, I doubt if ever they were of any use. He described the site and initial funding This place was selected by the deputation in 1822 for a small quay, and £250 appropriated to it. I laid out the works in the vicinity of the innermost of the old jetties and left a workman there who had been employed at Killough Harbour. He began it very substantially in hewn limestone, and proceeded some time by using day labour. The funds, however, were inadequate, and though some aid was obtained from the public,

the work was suspended for a season or so, and ultimately finished by contract."

The local landlords who in 1789 were prepared to invest in the infrastructure were no longer prepared to use their own money. In his report in 1825 he went on to describe how successful the development of the harbour appeared to be;

"The quay is now neatly built in hewn limestone, one hundred and five feet along the shore, with a return of seventy-two feet for boats, and jetty pier-head of seventy feet, extending to low water, with a good parapet. This pier is fifteen feet high and admits coasting vessels. A great deal of business is done here in shipping corn, landing turf, and in the fisheries. A packet sails regularly in summer to Galway and some good houses have been built at the quay; the wharf is commonly filled with craft."

Nimmo also recommended that public funds should be invested in building a road from New Quay or Burrin Quay (as it was also called) to Doolin and Liscannor as according to him the *"Burrin is in great want of an improved road"* as *"the current road is just a bridle road."*.

Alhough he made friends among the landed gentry, Nimmo also had many disputes when the local landlords' interests conflicted with what he saw as the best use of the government resources to help the poor. He insisted that labourers be paid cash rather than "an amount", which was a practise whereby they would get credit from the landlords for their labours, which would go towards their rent. Only with cash would the labourers be able to buy food. The Blakes in Connemara complained that he would not authorise funds to build a road, but Nimmo's response was that the road through the Blake estate would benefit the family but no one else. When Arthur French St George requested public funds for the repair and alteration of the road from Galway to Kinvara, Nimmo refused the allocation accusing

St George of desiring the work only so that his tenants would be employed, and the money would be used to pay him rent. In many of his reports he was scathing of the absentee landlordism and the poverty encountered as a result. In 1829 Nimmo was removed from his position and another engineer by the name of O'Donnell was given the task of completing the quay construction work along the western coast.

In 1833 O'Donnell presented the following to the Commission for Public Works regarding the state of New Quay harbour.

"A great deal of business was done here, and some good houses were erected on the shore. A substantial and useful work, but sometimes too small to contain the numerous craft seeking shelter in it. About 30 hookers and 150 yachts frequent the quay giving employment to 500 people in the fisheries. Large quantities of corn, butter, pigs, and sheep are regularly shipped here. In bad weather up to 100 crafts are known to take shelter here. I place it in the second class, as a mere fishery harbour, but for general utility it stands in the first class." So, while New Quay may never have achieved the hoped-for status as a fishing harbour, initially envisaged by Persse and Skerrett, it undoubtedly benefitted trade across Galway Bay and inland."

In 1837 in County Clare: A History and Topography, Samuel Lewis wrote:

"The small port of New Quay is situated about a quarter of a mile to the north of the village of Burren; a constant intercourse is kept up with Galway, on the opposite side of the bay, and a considerable trade in corn and fish is carried on; the boats employed in the Galway Bay fishery rendezvous here, and more than 100 of them have at one time taken shelter in stormy weather. The port affords great facilities for commerce, as vessels of considerable burden can

approach at any time of the tide: the coast is well adapted for sea bathing."

All the reports and eyewitness accounts from the period indicate that the area prospered and benefited from the trade resulting from the new harbour. However, during the famine period, the Poor Law commissioners sent to assess the status of the country, commented that the seas around North Clare were empty. The fishermen had sold their boats and nets to buy food, trade had dried up, so that those who had benefitted from casual labour to supplement their income and their meagre diet of potatoes now had no means to buy food or pay the rent.

Tourists

With the development of the quay, the popularity of the Flaggy Shore as a holiday resort for the gentry continued with frequent references in the society columns to the summer occupants in various houses and lodges. Reverend Hyacinth Skerrett (great grandson of his namesake who had petitioned for funding in 1789) with J Bagot (the leaseholder of Mount Vernon) tried to get funding in 1883 to build a brand-new quay opposite Harbour Hill House. A steamer that sailed between Galway and Ballyvaughan had run aground in New Quay and the owners no longer included it as a stop as they regarded the quay built in the 1820's as dilapidated. However, Skerrett and Bagot's request for funding was not successful and the pier from the 1820's still stands today.

13. 1836 Drawing of New Quay by TL Cooke. (By kind permission of County Clare Library)

7. The Tales of Red Bank Oysters and Burton Bindon

Trá Rua

In Aughnish Bay when the tide goes out a number of islands appear to the light and air, the size of the islands visible depends on how low the tide gets. During spring tides, it can sometime look like more land than sea, but everything gets submerged again with the incoming tide. One such island is Trá Rua, lying between Munnia and Doorus, a strip of land with a reddish hue that can be reached on foot from the seashore during the low spring tides. Trá Rua is translated as the Red Strand or, more famously the Red Bank, origin of the renowned oysters with the same name. In 19th century Dublin's finest taverns, frequented by the gentry and nobility, oysters sourced from the Trá Rua, Red Bank, were regarded as one of the most coveted items on the menu, described by one as follows: *"On trial they will be found to possess that briny flavour, with shortness, sweetness, and condition, which renders them one of the greatest and most nutritious delicacies—they should be eaten immediately after being opened, otherwise they lose that peculiarity of taste which they possess."*

The fondness for Red Bank oysters goes back further. The Inchiquin Papers Collection record that in August 1735, Sir Edward O'Brien, the 2nd Baronet, leased the lands at Rossrawley and Munnia to Bartholomew McNamara. Under the terms of the lease McNamara got the land for 8 years in return for an annual rent of £70 together with 20 horse loads of oysters, to be delivered to Dromoland Castle, each year, from these same oyster beds. The Earl of Inchiquin retained the freehold of the lands of Abbey parish following the Cromwellian Wars, but in 1750 Lord Inchiquin sold the lands of Munnia, Rossrawly and Currenrue to Francis Bindon. The sale included the nearby oyster beds.

The Bindons

Francis Bindon (c.1690 – 1765) was from a wealthy Protestant Ascendancy family that had been granted lands in Clooney, County Clare, and Limerick city in 1668. Living off the income from his estates, he led a privileged life, travelling and studying in Europe. He achieved fame first as a portrait painter and his portrait of Turlough Carolan (the blind harpist), hangs in the Irish National Gallery. Other portraits include four paintings of Dean Jonathan Swift, (dean of St Patrick's cathedral Dublin and author of Gulliver's Travels), who described Francis Bindon as "the greatest painter and architect of his time in these kingdoms". When his sight began to fail, it was said "he threw away his pencil" and Bindon concentrated on architecture. He is credited with the design of a number of significant buildings in Ireland including several country houses built in what was known as the classical style, a style he became familiar with during his travels to Rome.

In 1765 Francis Bindon died suddenly in his chariot on his way from Dublin to his estate in Clare. Francis hadn't married and had no children. He left his house in Dublin to his companion Francis Ryan and his estates in Clare passed to his brother Nicholas. Two of Nicholas's brothers, Samuel, and David, served as MPs in Clare. His other brother Thomas was Dean of Limerick and his sister Mary married George Roche Mayor of Limerick. By 1810 the Clooney estate and the lands in the Burren were in the possession of Burton Bindon, Nicholas's grandson. Burton, unlike his forebears who had followed artistic, legal, academic, and political careers, put his energies and money into developing the estates and shorelines that he had inherited, the results of which are still visible today.

Although the family seat was Clooney House near Bunratty, Burton Bindon spent most of his time in the Burren, where he lived first at Munnia Lodge and later at Currenrue House. In the lists of Clare Freeholders from 1821, he is recorded as owning land at Currenrue, Munnia, Rossrawley and New Quay as well as land in townlands around Clooney.

Land Improvements

In 1842, the antiquarian T. L. Cooke wrote a series of articles about his visit to New Quay and Currenrue including the home of Burton Bindon. In those, he spoke glowingly about Burton Bindon and the improvements he had made to the area, including converting land which had been sheer rock into fertile fields. The changes included the development of a conduit to pipe water down from Abbey Hill to a fountain at the roadside between Munnia and Rossalia. The land, from Corker Hill to Cartron, he cleared and laid out in strips comprising 20 acres each, separated by straight lines of double stone walls between the road and the sea. The double stone walls, still evident today, identified the boundaries between the lands leased to tenants.

The Bealach Duine, the steep hill from Munnia to Ballyvelaghan, was originally a narrow boreen. Bindon developed this into a road to make it easier for the men to take his horses to be watered at the lakes at the bottom of the hill. While seaweed and farming were important sources of income, the area of business which Bindon Burton is best known to have made his mark is the cultivation and trading of the Trá Rua Red Bank oysters.

Oysters

In the first half of the 19th century Bindon's oyster's industry offered the main chance of employment for many around New Quay, Currenrue and adjoining parishes. According to the testimony he gave in 1843 to the Devon Commission, as well as employing many men, he employed around 150 women during the oyster season, 1st of September to 1st May. The women worked from 11 a.m. to 2 p.m. each day at a rate 3d a day to process the oysters. In their hunger for employment, many of them travelled miles each day to earn their few pence. The oysters were brought from Kilkerran and Rossmuc Bays in Galway and were laid down to fatten on the Red Bank oyster bed for up to 7 years according to Bindon. He claimed in his testimony that he was the main trader of oysters from Tralee to Belmullet and at one time had given employment to over 20,000 people. He owned a boat called the Red Bank Lass that he used to sail from Currenrue around Galway Bay to pick up the young oysters along the west coast for bedding and maturing locally.

In the 1820s he requested funding from the Department of Public Works to build a quay at Currenrue, but when that wasn't forthcoming, he funded and built a quay and harbour there himself. In the Autumnal Rambles Cooke wrote of Bindon's endeavours at Currenrue as follows:

> *"In common with everything in this neighbourhood, owes much to the enterprising spirit of its owner. He has caused to be set up several*

sea and landmarks, with red flags attached to them, and serving as guides to direct the mariner through the safe and deep channel: he has also constructed at his own expense a quay-wall and harbour at Currenrue. The walls of this quay are built of immense squared blocks of limestone. — The facing and general execution of the work are so perfect that it would reflect credit on the most experienced government engineer or scientific builder."

In 1831 Burton Bindon proposed an ambitious plan to develop a route between Limerick and Galway to reduce the travel time to 6 hours. The route involved a road between Sixmilebridge and New Quay and a steamer service from New Quay to Galway.

"The Memorial to the Lord Lieutenant for a direct line of road between Limerick and Galway by Sixmilebridge and Newquay in Burren, on to the Bay of Galway, to accomplish the journey in six hours, has received the signatures of 14 of the County Limerick Magistrates, and a number of merchants and traders. —Part of the plan is to start a steamer from Newquay to Galway. The proposed plan has been surveyed, and laid out by Burton Bindon, Esq."

However, there is no evidence that the Lord Lieutenant gave any funding to develop the route and in the 1830's Bindon invested his own money in building the road known as the New Line, originally known as Bindon's Line, between New Quay and Crusheen. This enabled him to speed up the transport of oysters to the markets of Limerick, Dublin, Cork and to Rosslare.

Not content with sourcing and shipping his oysters, he also opened restaurants in Dublin where his oysters were the main item on the menu. In the 1830's Bindon owned first an Oyster Tavern at 17 & 18 Duke St in Dublin, and later in the 1840s, he set up a restaurant in 18 D'Olier Street, called the Red Bank Restaurant. His restaurants were regarded as among the most superior dining halls in Dublin, where the star attraction was the Red Bank oysters. The oysters won many plaudits at the time, as the quality was regarded as second to none. There were deliveries to Dublin from Currenrue, every second day in season and they were, according to his advertisements in the Dublin papers, transported, by water carriage. As the railway system didn't extend to the west, Limerick, or Galway, until the 1840s, transport was along the Shannon and canal system or by public road. Bindon was very protective of the reputation of his oysters. He claimed that the combination of red sand, salt and fresh water gave them their unique flavour. He quite frequently placed advertisements in newspapers threatening action against anyone purporting to sell Red Bank oysters,

In 1835 Bindon placed the following in the *Dublin Evening Post*:

"RED BANK OYSTER STORE, LUNCH AND SUPPER ROOMS, No. 17, DUKE-STREET

I do hereby caution the Public against the imposition which at present practised by certain persons who are retailing Oysters in Dublin, who are representing by placards and otherwise, that they have Red Bank Burren Oysters for sale, and whereas there are no Red Bank Oysters to be had at any other house in Ireland for retail but 17, DUKE STREET, DUBLIN, and Swinburn's Hotel, Brunswick Street, Limerick.

I also caution those persons from assuming the name or character of being connected with my Establishment, as I am determined to prosecute such persons with the utmost rigour of the law for such imposition and falsehood. BURTON BINDON.

The Public are respectfully informed that the above House has been established by the Proprietor of those extensive banks, and that no expense will be spared in forming the establishment on the same principle of the London Houses in neatness, attention, and extensive accommodation.

A large saloon together with several other separate distinct

apartments are already fitted for the reception of one hundred persons. The briny flavour and high condition of those oysters this season surpasses any specimen heretofore offered for sale, having been seven years transplanted, and fed on those Banks. N.B They are sold at 5s. per hundred, and sent out to every part of Dublin, carriage free".

Bindon, The Man

It would be difficult to overstate Bindon's s abilities as an entrepreneur and innovator. At a time when many of his counterparts were spending the rent they got from their estates on palatial style homes, Bindon poured most of his wealth back into the lands, seashore and developing the oyster markets. He invested heavily in land reclamation and development of the sea resources. In many ways by today's standards Bindon could be regarded as a harsh and merciless employer and even for the time the meagre wages he offered could be considered as paltry and miserly. The 5 shillings he charged for a hundred oysters would have paid 20 women for their days labour. But for the poor, the pennies he paid quite often made the difference between eating and starvation. In his testimony to the Devon Commission in 1843 he told the interviewers that having only a small family he had devoted his life to the interests of the poor.

When Daniel O'Connell was elected the first ever Catholic MP standing for Clare in 1829, it was said that most of the Protestant gentry left town and were not to be seen. Bindon was one of just six Protestant gentry that joined the throngs in the Sheriff's Offices and streets in Ennis to celebrate and to show their support. He was a noted horseman. It is recorded locally that with Bindon Scott (also a landlord in the Burren and cousin of Burton Bindon)_he organised horse racing on Munnia strand in 1818 where both he and Bindon Scott acted as stewards. He held a licence to keep a pack of hounds at Currenrue. Cooke, in The Autumnal Rambles describe him thus:

> *"One of the subjects best calculated to excite the surprise of the initiated in the neighbourhood of New Quay, is to behold this gentleman, mounted on his favourite hunter, with the hounds in full cry, and running at view before him, while he skims, like the light mountain breezes, over crags and down abrupt precipices, seemingly beyond the path of man."*

The double stone walls he had built in Munnia and Rossalia included creeps or low gaps where the hounds could pass through during the hunt. Cooke and others also spoke of his hospitality and generosity to visitors to his Currenrue home.

> *"THE NEW QUAY. In all my travels round the western coast I have not met anything equal to this as a watering-place: the scenery cannot be surpassed in point of beauty. You have here the advantage of sailing, fishing, shooting, and boat-racing, in the inlets of the bay of Pouldoody; and in the season, Red Bank oysters, of the most superior flavour and quality. On Saturday last I witnessed delightful sport on the much-improved demesne of Currenrue, the property of Mr. Bindon, who invited all the visitors here to join him in hare-hunting. and to the great delight of all present, his fine pack of hounds, after a sporting run of several hours, ran down three hares, one of which, from being hard pressed, escaped to the oyster bed. (The tide being out) when Mrs. Persse, on her splendid bay pony, and only a few of the sportsmen, were up at the death. The chase being over, the following distinguished families were invited by Mr. Bindon to partake of a dejeuner a la fourchette, which was tastefully laid out in the open fields :—Mr. and Mrs. Persse Roxboro; Hon. Mrs. Barry, Captain William Persse and Mrs. Persse, Carton Lodge ; Mr. and Mrs. Skerrett, Finavarra ; Misses Daly, Castle Daly; Mr. and Mrs. McMahon, and the Misses McMahon, Firgrove ; Mr. T. S. Cooke, and family, and the Misses O'Loughlin,*

of Port. The delightful day's amusement terminated with quadrilles, waltzes, and the national Irish Moneen jig."

But it wasn't just at Currenrue that he was famous for his lavish hospitality. The Journal of Irish hunting Notes from 1898 relating to hunting in the 1840s, gives details of the hunt breakfasts he hosted at Clooney. There he entertained the members who hunted with McMahon's of Firgrove. At the hunt breakfast any amount of flesh and fowl was served with copious amounts of Red Bank Oysters and washed down with all kinds of wine and tumblers of punch served from milk pails. As the members departed his home, he pressed them with horse loads of oysters and tumblers of punch.

Famine Years and Australia

In his testimony, Bindon told the Devon Commission in 1843 *"the population is increasing at such a rate but poverty also increasing that can only lead to a termination".* Sadly, the termination or catastrophe that he had prophesised was soon to pass when in 1847 Ireland was in the grip of the famine. According to the article below Bindon appeared to be one of the more sympathetic landlords during the famine years.

"A GOOD LANDLORD AND EMPLOYER. Burton Bindon, of Clooney, the County of Clare, Esq., proprietor of the extensive oyster banks, known at the Burren Oyster Bunks, has present in his employment 400 men and 300 women, engaged in collecting and dressing the oysters upon his properly, at the weekly wages of £190. The consequence which is, that there is no such thing known upon his estate, as a poor rate. A further instance of this gentleman's benevolence, it may be mentioned that upon Christmas Eve. Mr. Bindon presented his tenants upon his estate with 42lbs. of good beef, and a quantity of turnips, Christmas box, in

addition to their weekly wages. Such conduct cannot be too generally known or too highly commended."

Whether this is true or just propaganda is open to dispute as there are also frequent references in the press to the misery of the poor in New Quay. Notes from the Road Sessions he attended in the famine years show he opposed any Public Works including building new roads that would impact his property. He put forward the proposal that payments to the poor to till the land would be better use of funds available rather than building new roads. Father Fay, the parish priest in New Quay requested 400 tickets, i.e., requests for work, for 400 of Bindon's employees who were now destitute because of the famine. A traveller reporting in the Munster News in 1851 wrote of the *"woeful history of the tenancy evicted from the neighbourhood of Currenrue"*, a neighbourhood where Bindon was the main employer. There were also rumours that he was ignoring the destitution on his doorstep in Clooney by hiding away in Dublin, fearful for his safety.

By the middle of 1849, Bindon had decided the time was ripe to move on. He instructed an auctioneer to sell all the contents of Clooney House and stables including his animals, crops, and timber. The following advertisement was put in the paper: The Clare Journal, and Ennis Advertiser on Thursday 26 July 1849:

"Clooney County Clare. JAMES MARSHALL has been instructed by Burton Bindon, Esq. (who is about letting his various Farms), to Sell BY UNRESERVED AUCTION, at Clooney, (Within 13 miles of Limerick, 4 of Ennis, and adjacent to the Town of Quin), ON MONDAY, THE 6th OF AUGUST. All the Property thereat; likewise, a quantity of sundries removed from Currenrue for convenience of sale. The entire consisting of:

Six powerfully strong young draft horses, a strong Black Filly, 3 years old, Brown Filly, by Roscius. 3 off; Bay Colt, by Ernest, 3 off. unbroken; Scotch Drays, Carts, Tackling. Outside Car, Inside Car, Tax Cart on Patent Axes, Dog Van, Harness, 2 Side Saddles, same as new; Hunting Saddles, Bridles, 2 famous Spaniels, Wooden Gates, Iron Plough. Harrows, Turnip Machine Grinding stone; Ash. Elm, and Larch Timber; about 10 Tons of Rye Grass Hay; about 60 Acres of Meadowlng. most of which will cut and saved—the remainder sold in lots of about 4 acres; also, very superior highly bred Leicester rams.

The furniture consists of Drawing Room and Parlour Chairs. Two Sideboards, Large Chimney Glass, Pier Glass. Cabriolet Sofa, Sofa Table. 2 Handsome Round Tables. Card tables. Set of Dinner Tables, Drawing Room, Parlour and Stair Carpets. Large Sofa, Window Curtains. Fenders and Irons, Bookcase, Sofa Bed. Easy Chair, French, and other Bedsteads, with suitable Drapery; Feather Beds. Hair Mattresses. Blankets, Quilts, Bolsters, and Pillows; House Press, Dressing Tables, Basin Stands, Commodes, Bedside Stands. Clothes Horses. 8-day Clock, Hall Table, Butler's Tray, Drawers. 2 Chimney Lustres. Handsome Plated Epergne, 4 Corner Dishes and Covers, Plated Candlesticks and Snuffers, Cruet, Coasters. Ten Urns, 4 Dish Covers. Cake Basket. Knife Rests, Spoons, Forks. China; Dinner Ware. Cut Glass, Coppers, and Kitchen Requisites. All must be Sold in one day. an early attendance is solicited. The usual commission is chargeable to purchasers."

Two weeks later with the cash from the auction, Bindon was on his way to Australia. Sailing on board the Bolton from Plymouth, he was accompanied by four "Bindon girls". Two of those were his daughters and two were the daughters of his cousin Samuel Bindon (then living at Currenrue). Edward Snell, an English adventurer was on the same voyage and in his diaries commented that the "Bindon girls" were among the few interesting people on the ship. Bindon Burton was 73 years of age when he set off. His destination, South Australia was where several of the Clare Protestant landed gentry had made their home in the 1840s.

Captain Bagot, agent to Bindon Blood had arrived there on the Birman in the early 1840s with 400 Clare people. The discovery of copper in the early 1840's led to prosperity for many. However, by the time Bindon arrived the copper boom was coming to an end.

It is difficult to ascertain the main purpose of Bindon's trip; was he running away in fear, at a time when many landlords were fearful for their lives from those mercilessly evicted, or was it to seek his fortune like many who went to Australia at the time, or to find eligible men for the women he had bought with him? In Victorian times, with a shortage of eligible men at home in England, the gentry often embarked with their daughters to India and the colonies in search of husbands for their daughters. These trips were called "fishing expeditions." In post famine Ireland, when many of the gentry were in debt, Bindon may have thought his daughters' chances of finding eligible husbands were much better in Australia. If this was his goal, then Bindon certainly achieved his purpose. Arriving in Port Adelaide on the 29th of November 1849, three of the girls were married by 1852. His eldest daughter Ellen married Joseph Hall in 1850, in the city of Melbourne with Bindon and Jane Bindon (her cousin) as witnesses. Joseph Hall had emigrated from Armagh in the early 1840's, He was a successful businessman and owned an insurance company in Melbourne. Joseph already had a wife and a daughter when he married Ellen, but Bindon obviously didn't see this as being an obstacle to his being a suitable son-in -law. Jane Bindon married Henry Miller in the same church nine months later and Jane's sister Hannah Mazzey Bindon married Joseph Griffin in 1852. The fourth Bindon girl Elizabeth Bindon, Burton's daughter, was only 12 when they arrived in Australia, too young to be married off.

Return and Bankruptcy

Bindon, after spending just three years in Australia, returned home in 1852 with his daughters and new wealthy son-in-law in tow. Arriving back in Currenrue, one of his first actions was to sue John Scott in the Kinvara courts for taking the seaweed from the shores, while he had been away. With William Skerrett, he petitioned the authorities for a draw-bridge for the Muckinish to Finavarra ferry. But like many other landlords, after the famine, he couldn't ignore the debts that were accumulating and with his creditors clamouring for payment he was declared bankrupt. The Encumbered Estates Court forced the sale of his lands, in Rossrawley, Clooney, (including Clooney House,) Munnia and Currenrue. The properties were sold through the Encumbered Estates Courts in June 1853.

From the Freeman's Journal 8th June 1853:

"In the matter of the estate of Burton Bindon, Esq., owner, and petitioner. The fee-simple estate of said owner and petitioner in this matter, the lands of Clooney, situated in the barony of Bunratty, and the lands of Rossrawley, with its several denominations, together with the Red Bank Burren Oyster Beds, and the seaweed shore appurtenant thereto, situated in the barony of Burren, and said county of Clare, in the following lots, viz: - Lot 1.-The lands of Clooney, containing 603 statute acres, yielding a nett rental of 8481 1s 7d. The first offer was 5 0001, and Mr Orpen was declared the purchaser, in trust, for W B Fitzgerald, Esq, at 10,7001.

Lot 2-Roserawley and Currenrue, and the sea-weed shore adjoining same in the barony of Burren, containing 567 statute acres, and yielding a profit rent of 1751 10s 4d. The first offer was 1,0001, and Mr Guinness, in trust, was declared the purchaser at 8,500.

Lot B-Part of Munnia and the sea-weed shore adjoining same, in same barony, containing 237 statute acres, yielding a nett rent of 961 10s 3d. The first offer was 1,0001, Mr Guinness was declared the purchaser, in trust, at 1,775.

Lot 4.-Other part of same, with the Oyster Banks in same barony, containing 151 statute acres, yielding a profit rent of 823 14s 6d. The first offer was 1,0001, and Mr Guinness was declared the purchaser, in trust, at 2,7501."

However, Burton Bindon wasn't going to give up his oyster beds s without a fight.

'The Commissioner observed that an application had been made that the oysters of the present year should go to the credit of the estate; this could not, however, be done, as they should go to the purchaser, the commissioners not having power to separate them from the estate. Mr Guinness said that it was his intention to make a present of the oysters to Mr Bindon, on condition that they should go to himself and not to his creditors."

Following the sale Bindon's lands in the Burren became part of Colonel White's Estate, but Bindon still retained Munnia Lodge and 25 acres of land close by. He also connived to retain the oyster beds of Trá Rua because of the 'gift' from Mr Guinness, putting them beyond the reach of his creditors. He was forced to sell the premises at Duke St Dublin and though he fought against it, the premises at D'Olier Street, site of the Red Bank Restaurant, was also put up for sale.

Starting Afresh

Within three months of the sale of his estate and restaurants Bindon had opened a new "Red Bank Restaurant" next door to the previous one. He placed the following advertisement in the paper:

"The Red Bank Oysters Stores at 20, D'OLIER-STREET, DUBLIN, Opened on WEDNESDAY, the 21st instant. - The Proprietor of the Red Bank Oysters in the County of Clare,

late of 17, Duke-street, highly flattered at the unprecedented patronage given him by the Nobility, Military, and Gentry of Ireland, begs leave respectfully to announce that he has taken the very extensive premises, Nos. 19 end 20, D'Olier-street,' near Carlisle bridge, a few doors from Kinahan's Great Buildings, which are being fitted up in a style worthy of the company that supports him, and which kind a support contributes to the existence of several hundreds of a hard working race of people employed by him round the coasts of Ireland. No expense or trouble shall be spared in procuring the best articles, and rendering the house select and satisfactory as possible. This establishment does not open on Sundays. No. gambling or politics allowed. BURTON BINDON. Sept. 1853."

The records show that even having lost most of his estate, he was still living at Munnia Lodge and was active around New Quay. He took a local farmer Curtin to court and sued him for allowing sheep to trespass on his hay fields in Munnia. He contributed to a fund to raise money to build a Protestant Church in Ballyvaughan. He was also about to expand his oyster business. In January 1855, he opened a restaurant in Belfast, competing for business against local premises that were selling oysters from Carlingford Lough. He placed the following advertisement in the Belfast paper.

"THE STORMING OF BELFAST!! YES, I HAVE STORMED THE TOWN, with the powerful and invincible force of two hundred and thirty females employed by me daily on several Oyster Banks around the coasts of Ireland, give you, for what you now pay six and eight shillings, a superior Carlingford Oyster at four shillings per hundred, opened or unopened at 1/4d each. I came to lower the market to moderate and reasonable price, and let my laborious females live and let live, as 1 mean not to interfere with any man's concerns but mind my own, and do the best I can in a fair and reasonable way for myself, and put fifty per cent, in your pockets, AT No. 4, CASTLE STREET,

Which is, I conceive, full remuneration for walking a little more than one hundred yards to save two, and sometimes four shillings, on one hundred of Oysters. Look in, try once, and you can see and judge for yourselves applying to My Agent there. Spacious gas lighted rooms, with Lunch and Suppers always ready. Oysters forwarded to the country per order. The utmost exertions will made to make the company as select and respectable as possible. No gambling or politics allowed. The house does not open on Sundays. Respectfully yours, BURTON BINDON."

In 1856 he tried to get approval, through the Westport Courts to extend the oyster fishing season to include the month of May but he received a damning verdict. The following account of the hearing was reported;

"On Saturday last a respectable and numerously attended meeting was held at the Courthouse of this town (Westport). From the facts sworn on this occasion, it was quite evident Mr. Burton Bindon wanted to clear the bay of the small quantity of Oysters still in the banks. About 15 years ago he dredged four banks clear and now he wants to finish the work commenced, and not leave us a single Oyster. He cleared off Clew Bay 15 years ago and he has Connemara swept now and wants to return to Clew Bay again as a last resource. From the sworn evidence of interested parties, we sincerely hope he will be disappointed. He left the Court before the meeting separated and, I am credibly informed, without thanking the professional man engaged to conduct the case. (From Westport Court proceedings.)"

During the proceedings Bindon was blamed for the dearth of oysters in Clew Bay and along the Connemara coast due to dredging of the young oysters. His request to extent oyster fishing during the month of May was unsuccessful. The practice of leaving the oyster beds undisturbed from the 1st of May to end of August to allow the oysters to spawn had existed for centuries. In 1715 the Earl of Inchiquin had included in the leasehold agreement with R

Nugent for the lands of Rossrawley, a condition not to disturb the oyster beds from May to September.

Death and Legacy

Maybe it was due to the stress of the court case, but within a month of the hearing in Mayo, Bindon was dead, having died suddenly at D'Olier Street in Dublin. He was 79 years of age. His obituary was included in all the Irish and English newspapers of the day.

> *"Death of Burton Bindon, Esq— With feelings of sincere regret we must announce the sudden death, of Burton Bindon, Esq., of Munnia Lodge, County Clare, & D'Olier-street, Dublin, in 80th year of his age. The character of Mr. Bindon widely known as a true-hearted Irish gentleman, an excellent sportsman, and the proprietor of the Redbank Burren Oysters, renders all eulogy superfluous. All his numerous friends and acquaintances will deplore his loss." Galway Vindicator, 14th of June 1856.*

Bindon was survived by his two daughters, Elizabeth, and Ellen. He also fathered several illegitimate children; his name being recorded as their father in the Catholic baptismal records in Clare.

Two years following her father's death, Ellen returned to Clooney with her husband Joseph Hall and with his money, they purchased back the original home and estate, Clooney House and 630 acres of land. In 1858, they commissioned an eminent architect and builder to build a new house on the same site. No money was spared and when finished it was described as one of the finest mansions in Clare. In 1871 during a dinner party a fire started in the kitchen and the whole house was burned, the remains described as "just a pile of smouldering embers". They rebuilt the house and lived there until Joseph's death in 1906, followed by Ellen's 13 years later. They weren't very popular and there are thirty-three instances' cases in which Joseph Hall took the local people of Clooney to court for letting their sheep, cows, and geese trespass on his land. Joseph and Ellen lived extravagantly and when Joseph died it was said there was barely enough money left to bury him.

Elizabeth, Ellen's half-sister, married John Copley Singleton in December 1856, six months after her father's death. John Singleton was the second son of a Protestant landowning family who owned land around Quin, County Clare where their family seat was Hazelwood. Ellen inherited from her father, the house Munnia Lodge and lands at Munnia as well as the oyster beds and the D'Olier St restaurant. With her husband, she rebuilt Munnia Lodge and Elizabeth gave birth to a still born daughter there in August 1857 and a year later to a son in August 1858. The Electoral Rolls records show John Singleton as living in Munnia until 1870. The following article appeared in the Field newspaper on Saturday 7th January 1865, recounts a visit to the Red Bank oyster beds by its correspondent and shows that John Singleton took over where Burton Bindon had left off in running the oyster business.

> *"After about an hour's drive, we pulled up at a neat little cottage by the hill side, which has been built as a lodge by Mr Singleton, when he visits his property, for to him this Red Bank oyster-bed belongs, having succeeded Mr Burton Bindon in the property. Mr Singleton most fortunately happened to be down at the beds, and upon my introducing myself and Professor Melville, he not only paid us the greatest hospitality and attention but afforded us every facility for examining his oyster-beds."*

Describing the beds:

"The Red Bank Burren oyster bed is situated just in a bend of the Aughinish Bay, and here it is that oysters will fat to a greater extent than I believe almost any other known locality in Ireland."

His comments on the workers, show that many women still relied on the oyster beds for work.

"As we walked towards the shore, we observed a great many red-petticoated women trooping down the mountains side from different directions, these were the women Mr Singleton employs in the cultivation of his oysters.

The tide soon left the Red Bank uncovered, and as we walked about upon it I was exceedingly struck with the enormous quantities of oysters upon the ground: it was almost impossible to thrust the end of one's oyster-knife into the ground without touching and disturbing some of them; they reminded me, in fact, more of the appearance of a road newly covered with broken granite stones than anything else I can remember."

In the 1870s the Singletons put up for sale the Red Bank Restaurant at D'Olier Street and Munnia Lodge together with the remaining lands and seashore. The family moved to number 4 Ailesbury Road until 1890 when John died at Clooney House. Elizabeth was recorded in the census as living at Clooney Hall with Ellen in 1901 and 1911 and she died there in 1918.

Samuel Bindon, Burton Bindon's cousin continued to live at Currenrue House, renting the house and 11 acres of seashore from Colonel White until 1865. He inherited the Bindon estate at Waterpark but, like his cousin's estate, this was taken over by the Encumbered Estates Court. With no estate to inherit, all his family emigrated to Australia. On his death bed in Currenrue, although a Protestant, he asked the New Quay parish priest to give him the last rites and his last request was to be buried at Corcomroe Abbey. At the time he was the only known Protestant to have been buried there.

The Red Bank Restaurant in 19/20 D'Olier Street, continued to thrive as one of Dublin's most popular restaurants. Prior to World War II it became famous as the meeting place for the Irish Nazi Party. It finally closed its doors in 1969, having survived as one of Dublin's longest serving restaurants.

Meanwhile the island of Trá Rua continues to appear, exposed to the air, twice a day, before being submerged again by the incoming tide and if you are lucky, you may still find some of the fat succulent oysters for which the Red Bank has long been famous.

Section 5.
Crime and Punishment

8. The Tale of Peter Comyn

Introduction

When Peter Comyn of Murtyclough New Quay, was hanged from the gallows outside Ennis gaol in 1830, it sent shock waves through Clare. It was not because capital punishment or transportation for life were unusual sentences, in fact both were very common, an everyday occurrence for such punishments to be meted out to the lower classes, but it was almost unheard of for a member of the gentry, the ruling classes of the day, to suffer the same fate. The sentence of death by hanging of one of their own caused horror and consternation among the upper classes.

Who was Peter Comyn?

Peter Comyn was a member of the Clare gentry and through marriage was related to many of the wealthy and powerful families in Clare, Galway, and Limerick. His ancestor, John Comyn, was Mayor of Limerick in 1661, and married Margaret, daughter and co heir of the Kerry Park estate of Thomas Comyn. Following the Cromwellian transplantations, the Comyns lost their lands in Kerry but as innocent Papists (i.e., they had not rebelled against the British forces), they received in compensation, lands in the Burren. The lands, first acquired in Kilcorney, were taken from the O'Loughlin's who had been kings and rulers of the Burren since 12th century. The Comyn family later converted to Protestantism and expanded their estates throughout the 18th century by acquiring further lands in Ballyvaughan and Woodstock in Galway.

Peter Comyn was the son of David Comyn of Kilcorney and Dorothea McNamara of Doolin. Peter inherited land at Bishops Quarter from his mother and he also rented land at Murtyclough and Parkmore in the parish of Abbey and Oughtmama (now known as New Quay parish), from Bindon Scott. He became a magistrate and preventive coast officer (an arm of the coastguard service responsible for prevention of smuggling), serving Clare, Galway, and Limerick at various times. Having suffered bankruptcy, he was sacked from the magistracy and in the 1820's he was living in Scotland Lodge, a house in Murtyclough owned by Bindon Scott.

An 1823 map of the Bindon Scott estate in the parish of Abbey and Oughtmama includes Scotland Lodge and a Salt House rented to Peter Comyn. The Salt House was on the site of what later became Halloran's shop. Scotland Lodge was next to Burren village, which in the early 19th century was the centre of the parish with a Post Office and Constabulary.

14. Site of Salt House (taken from 1823 estate maps of Bindon Scott by kind permission of the NLI)

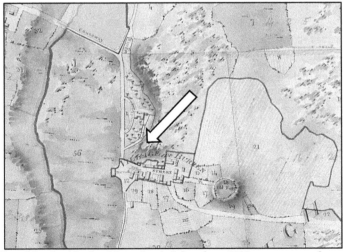

15. Site of Scotland Lodge Mortyclough (taken from 1823 estate maps of Bindon Scott by kind permission of the NLI)

Character of Peter Comyn

Peter Comyn was regarded as a strange and complex character prone to bouts of insanity. There was a lot of hostility between him and his landlord Bindon Scott, dating to a feud over land between the families from the middle of the 18th century. John O'Donovan in his letters describes him as *"affording a rare instance of human talent, honour, folly, and dishonesty most strangely combined in the one character."* He was reputed to have collected local legends and written a manuscript describing the habits, morals, and superstitions of the local people. He led what the newspapers later called "a free life" never marrying but having a common law wife and three, or possibly four, children.

In the mid 1820's he was one of only three Protestants living in the locality of New Quay. One of the other two was Peter Blake Morgan, widower of Mary Jane Skerrett. Letters to the undersecretary for Ireland, from Peter Morgan survive, in which he requests the reinstatement of Peter Comyn as magistrate on the basis that his dismissal was for a trifling revenue matter. Although Comyn claimed to have built Scotland Lodge himself, the freehold was owned by Bindon Scott of Cahircon. As the relationship deteriorated with his tenant, Scott gave him notice of eviction.

Fire at Scotland Lodge

On the 6th of December 1829 a fire broke out and Scotland Lodge was burned to the ground. According to Comyn, neither he nor his two servants, who lived there, were home at the time. At first news of the fire, all the papers were filled with sympathy for Comyn, having lost his home in what appeared to be an arson attack. The following was from the Kerry Evening Post on the 23rd of December 1829:

"On the night of Sunday, the 6th instant, some evil-disposed person, or persons set fire to, and totally consumed the commodious and beautiful house of Scotland Lodge in the Barony of Burren, and neighbourhood of Newquay, County Clare, the residence of Comyn, Esq. and for many years the most hospitable and beautiful place in Clare. Mr. Comyn, like many others in the present and fully depressed state of the times, was under some embarrassment and under dread of an impending execution. He had only removed himself that very evening from the house, on a temporary visit to friend in the neighbourhood; but, alas as the Monday morning dawned, Scotland Lodge was in flames, and is now a shapeless mass of ruins. Fortunately, Mr. Comyn and all his servants had left the house, else it is probable a loss of lives would now be deplored along with serious loss of property, as the house was not insured."

The struggle for Catholic emancipation and its achievement in 1829 with the election of Daniel O Connell as the first Catholic MP, demonstrated the power of political mobilisation of the masses. The rise of the Terry Alts (in protest at the changes from tillage to pasture farming and payments of tithes) was enabled in part using the same forces, but also wielded the threat of physical violence. So, at first glance, the attack on Comyn's home was perceived as possibly a sectarian attack against Comyn as a member of the Protestant landlord class. However, following an investigation by the local constabulary, the fire was found to be deliberate, and Comyn was suspected of being the culprit. He was arrested by the local constabulary and taken before the Magistrates Court, presided over by Burton Bindon, his friend and neighbour in Currenrue. At the same time, he also had a charge of forgery hanging over him. In the preceding Summer eight or nine magistrates had been sent letters of complaint against a local farmer John Hynes. The letters had been signed with a signature of James Hynes. When the complaints were investigated the local postman was able to recall seeing Comyn posting the letters and investigations revealed that the hand writing bore a remarkable similarity with that of Peter Comyn's.

Charge and Trial

On the 23rd of December Comyn was charged with arson and sentenced to be tried by jury. When the trial took place in March, Comyn was found guilty and sentenced to be hanged. The Kerry Evening Post. on Saturday 13 March 1830 reported the following:

> *"Mr. Comyn, for maliciously burning and two for burglary On Monday last, Peter Comyn, Esq. of Scotland Lodge, near Burren, was tried for having maliciously burned his house on the 6th of December last. The premises were under ejectment, and coming into possession of Bindon Scott, Esq. when the wicked deed was perpetrated. He was sentenced after a trial of seven hours. Sergeant Blackburne convinced a respectable Jury, and after a moment's consideration indictment was capitally laid. Mr. Comyn is allied with many respectable families, and was Magistrate, at times, for the counties of Clare, Galway, and Mayo."*

Appeal to The King

Following the sentencing, huge efforts were made by the Clare gentry to have the sentence of death commuted. An appeal was made to the Home Secretary and request for a pardon to His Majesty King George IV. On the 6th of April 1830, the Dublin Evening Post published the following: *"A memorial to his majesty was on Friday forwarded from Ennis in favour of Peter Comyn, Esq. under sentence of death from arson"*. It had been hoped that the king would give a sympathetic ear to a petition from the Protestant gentry of Clare who had opposed Catholic Emancipation. The king, George IV in 1928 had reportedly danced and jumped on his pen in fury when forced to sign the royal decree granting Catholic Emancipation which allowed Catholics to take their seat in parliament. The change in the law followed Daniel O Connells landslide victory when as a Catholic he stood as a candidate in the County Clare constituency. The king, suffering from declining mental and physical health, was either unable or unwilling to intervene. The request for pardon was not granted and his friends with the support of the press made a number of further attempts to have his sentence repealed.

Appeal Based on His Mental State

A woman from Bristol came forward with a letter Comyn had written to her which she claimed provided evidence that he was of unsound mind. Efforts were then made to use his mental state as a reason for clemency. The *Cork Constitution* published a letter including the following extract on Thursday 8th April *"It would be placing ourselves accessories after the fact, were to suppress any longer the conviction that this unfortunate gentleman is a fitter subject for the inner walls of a Lunatic Asylum than for the platform on which he was sentenced to expiate crime for the commission of which, men in possession of their reason should alone be accountable to the laws."* The paper went on to detail an instance in which Comyn, following a bout of *mental aberration,* had required four men to control him. An operation on his head had been performed, which provided some temporary relief, but he was still subject, as several people could vouch, to frequent attacks of insanity. The appeal was to the Lord Lieutenant to take his mental state into consideration. As evidence was produced of his poor mental state, a lunacy investigation *"lunatico inquirendo"* was requested. The following was posted on the 17th of April in the *Waterford Mail.*

"A government messenger came down specially yesterday morning with an order from the Lord Lieutenant to the High Sheriff of the county Clare, for staying the execution of Peter Comyn, Esq. to

Wednesday 28ᵗʰ. We understand a Commission "lunatico in-quirendo" has been issued to ascertain the state of mind Mr. Cornyn, and in order to afford time for arriving at a just conclusion on this point, it is that the respite had been sent down."

However, following the investigation the claims that Comyn was of unsound mind failed to carry weight. While, in the meantime, there were news reports that the King had requested the Irish Government to intervene to mitigate the sentence of capital punishment, these reports proved to be unfounded.

Appeal to The Catholic Clergy

Vesey FitzGerald, who had been the MP for Clare before being unseated by the Liberator Daniel O'Connell, suggested that an appeal be made by the Catholic clergy for Comyn's sentence to be commuted. FitzGerald was a Protestant, and it was felt that a Catholic clergymen's appeal would strengthen the case that the request to have his charge commuted had universal appeal across all religions. On Monday 12 April 1830 the Freeman's Journal published an article including the following extract:

"It may not be amiss to add, that as Mr. Comyn is a member of the Established Church, Mr. Vesey FitzGerald suggested the propriety of recommending that a petition should be presented on his behalf by the Catholic Bishop and Clergy, a request which was readily acceded to. We are glad this result has taken place as from the spirit now abroad to mitigate the severity of our criminal code, we are convinced that the law of arson could not last for a year longer without being rendered more conformable to public opinion." However, although Comyn had converted to Catholicism in the weeks

after his trial, this appeal was not sufficient to save him and any news to the contrary was unfounded."

Appeal by The Masses

His supporters believed that the refusal of the authorities to pardon him was so they would not seem to give preferential treatment to one of their own class at a time when sectarian strife was rife in the county. His supporters raised a petition getting the poor from his neighbourhood to sign on his behalf, believing that if the authorities could be persuaded that his release had universal approval, that this would strengthen his case for clemency. The following appeared in the Mayo Constitution on the 29 April 1830.

"MR. PETER COMYN. It is now apprehended notwithstanding all the cruel suspense which marked the progress of this unfortunate case that Mr. Peter Comyn is doomed to suffer the extreme judgement of the law. One of the reasons assigned for this determination on. the part of the Government is said to be, the injurious effect the exercise of clemency may bare on the feelings and opinions of the peasantry, from supposition that the indulgence of the Crown was in consequence of his rank and station in society but much to the credit of the peasantry of Clare, we understand the impression is quite different on their minds, for deeply affected, are they in his fate, and anxious to avert the sentence of the law, through a petition from them on his behalf is in process of signature through the entire county. It is therefore ardently to be hoped that Government will, in its wisdom and humanity give a listening ear to the prayers of the poor on this awful occasion."

Hanging Outside Ennis Gaol

However, even with the support of the people and a sympathetic press all the efforts to save him failed and on the 29th of April 1830, he was hanged outside Ennis New Gaol. The newspapers described in detail the proceedings of the days. Most of the local gentry left town beforehand and all the shops were shut. But this didn't stop the crowds, they thronged the streets from early dawn to see the spectacle, vying for the best views of the proceedings. He was accompanied to the gallows by two Catholic priests. The following description of his funeral was published in the *Limerick Evening Post* on Friday 30 April 1830.

> *"The body was lowered down and put into an elegant coffin richly mounted, and conveyed in a hearse, followed by a train of carriages and over five thousand persons, to outside the town. The principal part of the cavalcade accompanied the remains of Mr. Comyn to Corofin from whence they are to be removed for interment to the family vault at Madaboy, in the West of the County. All public offices and shops throughout the town of Ennis were closed, and the melancholy gloom to be met in every countenance showed how deeply and sincerely he was regretted."*

Conversion to Catholicism

The support and sympathy of the press proved short-lived. The day before the hanging, he had written a letter laying out his beliefs and conversion to Catholicism and requesting it to be published following his death. The following was the content of the letter:

Ennis Gaol, Half-past 2 o'clock 28th April 1830.

> *"Having attentively listened to the Clergymen and laymen of the different persuasions on the most important of all subjects, my eternal happiness, I am firmly convinced that the Holy Catholic Church is that in which I can more securely die. During the last month I hope have laboured to avail myself of the advantages and graces imparted by the Mother Church, exclusively, and with my last accents I leave my blessing to the Very Reverend and Venerable Dean O'Shaughnessy, the Chaplain of the*

*Prison, and to the Reverend gentleman whom he has selected to
administer spiritual consolation to my departing spirit.
James Fitzpatrick,
Ralph Cullinan,
James O'Shaughnessy*

PETER COMYN"

The next day the *Catholic Sentinel* published an article
entitled: *"Triumph of the Catholic Religion EXECUTION of
MR. COMYN, IN ENNIS, FOR FORGERY."* In the article they described the hours before his execution, waiting
in the prison, praying with six clergy in attendance as well
as three of his illegitimate children. The description painted
him as a pious almost Christ like figure, as he kissed each
member of the clergy on the cheek, resigned to his fate, as
he walked to his execution. The article also failed to mention the main crime for which he was found guilty that of
arson.

However, the general press that had been previously
sympathetic, took a very cynical view of the letter and his
late conversion to Catholicism. They saw it as a move by the
liberals, the pro Catholic emancipation forces, to gain Catholic sentiment. The Irish press now took to describing him
as a deluded character. *"So, Comyn who in younger life was a man
of property, worth six hundred a year and Magistrate of three Counties,
he had lived what the press called 'a free life' he had never married and
had 3 or 4 common law children. When he died at 52, he wasn't worth
one shilling."*

Following His Death

Scotland Lodge wasn't rebuilt, and no house has ever been
constructed on the site. The fortunes of his former enemy
Bindon Scott did not fare well in the years following
Comyn's execution. Mary Frances, Scott's only daughter and

heiress eloped to Gretna Green in Scotland with a Catholic, Maurice O'Connell, son of Daniel O'Connell. The families were later reconciled and there are frequent references to Daniel O'Connell holidaying in New Quay with the Scotts. When Bindon Scott died in 1837 much of his family's fortune had disappeared and most of the estates, he owned across County Clare had to be sold in the following 15 years.

Section 6.
Religion, Relics
and Ritual

9. The Tale of Corcomroe Abbey

Introduction

In 1990, when John O'Donohue, priest, poet and philosopher chose Corcomroe Abbey as the site for an Easter Sunday dawn Mass, he was rekindling an ancient tradition that stretched back to the earliest times of Christianity in Ireland. This was the start of a trend for Easter Sunday open air dawn masses in ancient abbeys and on beaches throughout Ireland and Corcomroe, the Cistercian abbey of Santa Maria de Petri Fertili long abandoned by the monks, set within the limestone mountains of the Burren, was an apt setting. It was a place close to the heart of John O'Donohue which he alluded to again and again in his writing.

Corcomroe certainly has its share of spirits. In its tumultuous history dating back 800 years it has served as the final resting place for kings, chieftains, warriors, bishops, and clergy as well as local poets, musicians, and the native people of New Quay and Bellharbour. But the story of Corcomroe, a story of mystery and contradictions, is more than a story of memorials for the dead.

Donal Mor O'Brien

The story and fortunes of Corcomroe Abbey are interwoven with the history of the O'Brien dynasty. Donal Mor O'Brien, last king of Munster is the main contender as the founder of the abbey sometime in the late 12th century. A descendant of Brien Boru and son in law of Diarmait Mac Murchada, (who first invited Strongbow and the Normans to Ireland), Donal Mor succeeded his father Toirdhealbhach to the kingship of Munster in 1168. His election as chief of the O' Brien dynasty was secured when he blinded two of his cousins in battle. Under Irish Brehon Law, being incapacitated prohibited a member of the kinship group (the derfine) from being elected chieftain. He was given the title "Donal Mor" meaning "Donal the Great" for his prowess in battle, but also for his patronage of the church.

Donal Mor is credited with the endowment of at least four new Cistercian abbeys in Munster and the re-endowment of Inisloughtan Abbey. The sites of the Cistercian abbeys, located like a string of pearl across the plains of Munster, were strategically selected in areas where he had battled for supremacy or where the territory was in contention with local chieftains. The stone abbeys, designed according to the Cistercian blueprint, were so vast and grand that 800 years later they still dominate the landscape. River location was an important criterion as fish placed a large part in the monastic diet and the Cistercian monks were noted for their hydraulic expertise as well as pioneering farming methods.

The choice of site at Corcomroe would seem at odds, existing as it does many miles from the rich plains of Munster. Yet the site is in a strategic location in the Burren, close to the Corker Hill, the historic routeway between Munster and Connaught. In the absence of rivers, proximity to the coast was crucial. The Cistercians built many abbeys near the coast, as well as access to fish and shellfish for the monks diet the location often allowed them to harness the power of the sea for building tidal mills for grinding corn. A tidal mill existed in Currenrue up until recent history. It's possible that the Cistercians were the first to build a mill here. The abbey location as the site of earlier skirmishes between the O'Briens and the O'Connors (lords of Corcomroe), was also significant. The O'Briens were encroaching on the territory of North Clare and the foundation of a new abbey was as much a mark of their control over local lordship as the patronage of the churches for their own salvation. Donald Mor died in 1194 and recording his death the Annals called him: "A refulgent torch of peace and war and the brilliant star of hospitality and generosity of Munster".

Donnchadh Carbreach O'Brien

While the circumstantial evidence points to Donal Mor as the founder, no documentary proof exists. What we do know is that a contingent of 12 monks and an abbot (the numbers defined by the Cistercian rule), left Inisloughtan Abbey in county Tipperary and travelled to the Burren and founded a new daughter monastery on land granted to them by the O'Briens. So, while Donal Mor may have granted the land to the Cistercians, the actual building of Corcomroe Abbey was probably built under the lordship of his son Donnchadh Carbreach O' Brien. Stalley the archaeologist has pointed to a date of 1200 – 1205 for the earliest part of the abbey based on the architectural style and comparison with other sites. The earliest documentary evidence relating to Corcomroe is a charter dated 1224 from Dijon in France under which Donnchadh Cairbreach agrees to provide an annual payment of two marks of silver to the Cistercian mother house Citeaux Abbey in France. The charter is witnessed by among others the Cistercian abbot of Corcomroe (de Petra Fertili). Another charter which exists with the seal of Donough Cairbreach, contains the account of annual offerings promised by 12 local Munster chieftains and their wives all who promise a rent of 12 denarii but having no seals of their own, at their request the king affixed his own seal to the charter.

The Cistercians

The entrepreneurial spirit of the Cistercians and their innovative farming and fishing methods meant that the O'Briens and other nobles from Ireland and Europe fell over themselves donating lands and money for new communities and abbeys. The Cistercian order, founded at Citeaux near Dijon in France in 1098, was the most remarkable of the European monastic movements of the 12th century. Its emphasis on a return to an austere life and literal observances of the rules set out for monastic life by St Benedict in the 6th century, were seen by other monks of the time as being 'the surest road to heaven'. One of the main features in early Cistercian way of life was the emphasis on manual labour and self-sufficiency through working the land. All monks were required to do some manual labour as part of their daily ritual. Colonies of monks were sent out from Citeaux and founded mother houses and then daughter houses across Europe, leading to the creation of a network of Cistercian monasteries that were bound together in unity and uniformity in the Cistercian way of life and worship.

It is said that Saint Malachy, bishop of Armagh was on his way to see the Pope, when he stopped off in Clairvaux. He was so impressed with the Cistercian way of life that he asked the Pope, Innocent II, if he could become a Cistercian monk. The Pope wasn't having any of it and sent him home to continue the reform of the Irish church, aligning it more closely with Rome. When Malachy stopped off again in

Clairvaux, on his way home, he left behind some of his companions to be trained as Cistercian monks and when he returned to Armagh, he persuaded some more of his clerics to go to France and join them. So, when the first Cistercians appeared at Mellifont, in 1142 at the invitation of Malachy, their number consisted of a few Irish as well as French monks. From Mellifont the monks were sent to colonise daughter houses across the country. In Munster the first monastery was at Monasteranagh, Mainister near Croom in Limerick, built under the patronage of Toirdhealbhach Mac Diarmada O'Brien king of Munster and father of Donal Mor. Their economic prosperity in Munster in the 13th century was in large part attributed to sheep rearing and wool production for export.

The Cistercians' belief in simplicity and austerity extended to their buildings. Unlike other orders, the Cistercians prescribed that the style of architecture in the abbey should be plain and unadorned with minimal decoration and follow strict guidelines on layout. There should be no distractions for the monks in their houses of prayer through use of decoration. The aspiration was that monasteries were so uniform that a monk coming from a Cistercian house anywhere would feel quite at home in one of the other monasteries. Most of the monasteries were dedicated to the Blessed Virgin and many given a name starting with Santa Maria. Corcomroe was called "Santa Maria de Petra Fertili"- "St. Mary of the Fertile Rock" reflecting the fertile nature of the Burren lands, which may not be immediately obvious to someone looking across the bare limestone. It later became known as Corcomroe Abbey at a time when the Barony of Burren was known as East Corcomroe.

Corcomroe Abbey followed the Cistercian custom of being in an isolated place away from the world, where the monks were required to be self-sufficient but generate a surplus from farming to be paid to the mother house. The overall design, and placement of different buildings within the abbey followed the Cistercian plans, with defined areas for prayer, work, dining sleeping, study etc. However, the style and decoration in Corcomroe could certainly not be described as austere and simple. While the architecture of many Cistercian foundations throughout Ireland reflected their desire for austerity and purity as well as their disapproval of ornament, those in the west, farthest removed from English and Norman influence, appear to have had their own ideas, influenced by the grand ambitions of their patrons. In Corcomroe the artistic range of the stone carvings, including the delicate herringbone and chevron ribbing of the vault of the presbytery were in contradiction to the strict austerity of the Cistercians. The earliest parts of the abbey to be constructed were the eastern and northern sections which included the presbytery. The rib vaulted chancel and finely carved capitals show evidence of the finest detail of workmanship. The decoration includes intrinsic carvings of dragons, human heads, and flowers. The delicacy of the floral carvings is unique; the depiction of flowers in stone is not seen anywhere else in this period. The Burren, famous for its flowers, might seem an appropriate place, yet the flower carvings depicted were not wildflowers of the Burren, but resembled more exotic plants, probably introduced from France, or grown for medicinal purposes.

The architectural style adopted, often referred to as the 'School of the West' is evident in other contemporary stone churches and monasteries west of the Shannon. Work carried out by a group of stone carvers, sculptors and masons using similar decorative detail are evident in Killaloe Cathedral, Knonkmoy and Boyle Abbey as well as at Kilfenora and Kilmacduagh and in the largest church at Oughtmama, suggesting that the same the group of masons were involved in each. The fact that the style is contrary to the Cistercian architecture is probably an indication of the influence of the patrons, led by the O Brians and other nobility of North Munster and Connaught who sponsored decoration and artistic displays as a reflection of their own status in the grand church buildings they endowed.

The detail from the stonework on the east and north sections of the abbey, show that it was carried out by expert craftspeople, but what has puzzled historians and archaeologists is the fact that the west and south sections show that the work on those sections was completed without any of the same attention to detail. There are clear indications that the building work was halted and when restarted rougher stonework was used, the carvings are missing and mistakes in masonry are obvious, as well as signs that certain parts of the abbey were never completed, or were missing entirely, for example the northern aisle.

The evidence suggests that the initial foundation started with ambitious plans to build a splendid building, but long before this programme was complete, something went wrong, and the work stopped. A number of reasons have been proposed including shortage of money or famine. But the most likely reason is probably the change in control within the Cistercian order and transfer of the mother house from Inisloughtan Abbey to Furness Abbey in Lancashire.

The events that led to the change in control started with an internal reform movement within the Cistercian order which included efforts to bring the Irish abbeys back into line. Stephen Lexington was abbot of Stanley, a Cistercian monastery in England, when he was commissioned to go to Ireland as a delegate from the General Chapter to reform the Irish monasteries. In line with the policy of maintaining centralised control, the abbot of each Mother House in Europe was required to travel each year to Citeaux to attend the Annual General Chapter on or around Holy Cross Day on the 14 September. This was an event at which Cistercian legislation, disciplines and penalties were set down according to the Cistercian constitution. Letters from Citeaux have survived from 1227, 1228 and 1229 with complaints that the Corcomroe abbot did not show up at the Annual General Chapter. This was not just a Corcomroe problem but extended to many of the Irish monasteries. When Stephen Lexington came to Ireland in 1228 there were 10 French speaking Anglo-Norman Cistercian monasteries and 21 native monasteries, most still under the Mellifont mother house and those he highlighted for reform. Among the problems he identified were lack of observance to the rule, too much idle chatter, too much eating and drinking, too much concern for personal belongings and too much contact with the outside world, including with women. He drew up a long list of rules and regulations to be strictly followed by the Irish Cistercian monks. He forbade people from leaving the abbey and forbade women past the gate. He specified that only those fluent in French and Latin could become monks and bought in French and English abbots to replace the Irish. Unsurprisingly his changes were met with resistance in many abbeys.

When he visited Inisloughtan (the mother house of Corcomroe) he was met with violent opposition from the monks. When they heard of his imminent arrival, they hid in the nunnery buildings and ambushed him. In Maigue or Monasternanagh, the monks led by their abbot, expelled the English abbot he had installed and barricaded themselves in the abbey, turning it into a fortress and armed themselves with stones. Stephen Lexington didn't visit Corcomroe, but he allowed Corcomroe, like Knockmoy and Boyle in Connaught, to elect an Irish abbot. He affiliated Corcomroe to the rule of Furness Abbey in Lancashire. The arrival of Stephen Lexington could also be seen as having a political agenda. The period coincided with the desire of the English authorities to extend their control in Ireland and while the O'Brien kings reigned in Munster, that task was made more difficult. Donnchadh Carbreach's nephew, the abbot of Monasteragh, was one of the leading rebels against the change in control. Stephen Lexington's correspondence shows that he clearly didn't trust Donnchadh Carbreach and saw him as the ringleader who resented the presence of the Anglo-Normans in Ireland. The conclusion was that the reform movement (which started with the introduction of French and Norman influence), meant that Corcomroe was now obliged to follow a more austere and simpler lifestyle. This may have hurried up the completion of the abbey at Corcomroe with less money to spend on fine finishing.

But the complaints didn't go away. In the Cistercian decrees of 1270-1274, nearly fifty years, later several complaints were made regarding the lack of discipline in certain Irish monasteries including Corcomroe. In 1274, Archbishop David of Cashel, also a Cistercian, persuaded the General Chapter at Citeaux to restore all the daughter houses to Mellifont's jurisdiction. Then, according to the English commentator William of Neburgh, "they went back to their bad old ways."

Conor Siudane

Donnchadh Cairbreach, king of Thomond, was succeeded by his son Conaire Rua O'Brien in 1242. Conaire, also known as Conaire Siudane was successful in pushing back against the De Clare Normans who were encroaching on Thomond. However, after his son was killed in battle, he became apathetic and depressed and was said to have lost his zeal for fighting and no longer wished to be king.

A Cistercian charter believed to date from the 1250's signed by Conaire Siudaine, and his wife Annalusia, agreed to pay 2 silver marks to Citeaux every year as a continuation of the charter signed by his father in 1224. The relationship between Conaire Siudaine and the Cistercian order was typical of many between those who were patrons, and the order. In return for their patronage, the Cistercians provided their princes with spiritual benefits. The prayers of the monks acted like a powerhouse used for the salvation of their patrons' souls and those of their family. The charter effectively gave Conaire Siudaine and his wife confraternity with the entire Cistercian order, ensuring them the level of intercession for their souls afforded to a Cistercian monk. Favours often, as in the case also of Conaire Siudaine, extended to burial within the monastery close to the altar, which was otherwise reserved to members of the order.

It may have been that his enemies, including the other O'Brien factions, saw Conaire Suidane's despondency as a sign of weakness and the attacks on his territories increased as his enemies formed against him. This culminated in a battle in the Burren in 1268 involving the O'Loughlins, the local chieftains, and other O'Brien factions siding with them against Conaire. Conaire Siudaine along with members of his family (his son, daughter, and grandson) and supporters were killed in the battle near Corcomroe Abbey. The annals of the Four Masters state:

> "The age of Christ, 1268. Conor Roe O'Brien, Lord of Thomond, Seoinin, (i.e., little John) his son, his daughter, his daughter's son, i.e., the son of Rory O'Grady, Duvloughlin O'Loughlin, Thomas O'Beollan, and a number of others, were slain by Dermot, the son of Murtough O'Brien, for which he himself was afterwards killed; and Brien, the son of Conor O'Brien, then assumed the lordship of Thomond."

The Annals of Inishfallen also records that the army lead by Conaire na Siudaine, advanced through Clare where they were joined by members of the O'Dea and O'Hehir families. History records they went to the upper Canthred (the Burren) to bring the inhabitants there to submission. They burned the country north of Duibh-Gleann (includes modern townlands of Oughtmama and Turlough) and proceeded northwards to Béal-Clogaidh (Bellharbour), near the sea, where they were met by Conor Carrach O'Loughlin and his allies, and a battle ensued in which Conor na Siudaine O'Brien together with a great many of his people were slain by O'Loughlin and the race of Donnell Conachtach O'Brien. Conor na Siudaine was buried by the monks in the Abbey of Corcomroe and his family members were buried beside him.

Conaire was given the name Siudaine, and it has been said that he is so called because he was killed in a place called Siudaine Woods. Siudaine may be a corruption of Saoi Duine, literally translated as a 'Wise person" or" Monastic person or people". There may have been woods owned by the monks close by where he was killed. or the name could have been given to him from his patronage of the Cistercians with whom he was laid to rest. Today his tomb and stone effigy survive and lie in the north wall of the presbytery of the abbey. The following description of the effigy is provided in the Clare County Library website:

"It shows the King wearing a crown decorated with fleur de lys, the left hand holds a sceptre and the right a reliquary suspended from the neck of the figure. His robe falls in long pleats to below the knee while the figure appears to lie on a cloth with the feet resting on a cushion."

The effigy is one of the oldest surviving effigies of an Irish chieftain. A very similar one is found in Roscommon Friary. That is a memorial to Felim O'Connor, a former king of Connaught (and an old enemy of Conaire O'Brien) who having resigned as a king joined a monastery and died as a monk in the Friary some years earlier than Conaire Siudaine, in 1265.

1317 Battle

In 1317 the abbey was again at the centre of the wars caused by the internal feuding of the O'Briens as different branches of the family fought for dominion of Thomond. This time the conflict included the Norman family De Clare, who tried to make inroads into the Thomond territories. A battle took place at a spot called Druim Lurgain, (translated as the shin shaped ridge), believed to be close by Muckinish, with the heads of most of the principal families in Thomond aligned on one side or the other.

The O'Brien family historian described the lead up and the battle in the Cathreim Thoirdhealbhaigh, (Triumph of Turlough), a document dated from the 15th century. Translated by Hayes Standish O'Grada (in 1929), the story of the battle highlights the relationship between the monks of Corcomroe and their patrons the O'Brien kings. It shows how far the lives of the monks had veered from the simple austere life locked away from the distractions of the world envisaged by their founder St Bernard but also the extent of their support and loyalty to their patrons.

The night before the battle Donough Mac Donall Mac Brien Rua (the O Brien king and chieftain), had been lavishly entertained in the Corcomroe Abbey by the Cistercian monks. In the morning, having slept in sumptuous luxury he with his followers attended Mass. It was the feast of the Assumption, the 15th of August. Then, rallying his supporters from the various Irish factions and local lordships, Donough Mac Donall and his followers armed themselves and accompanied by the 'warrior monks' (the cullenachs), prepared for battle:

> *"Donough was armoured; and together with his warrior-monks and Maccon issued from the Abbey, and a strange sight it was to see those Cullenachs (unkempt individuals) come tumbling out and wriggle on their harness as they ran; nor ever, out of any monastery*

whatsoever, had there streamed an order [of friars] more grimly bent on fighting for their lands."

Passing close by Lough Rask on the way to the battle ground, Donough and the men were met by the sight of an old crone. Described as *"distorted and loathsome"*. She arose from the lake and made dire predictions, foretelling that the O'Brien leader along with many of his kinsmen would lose their heads before the end of the day. Dismissing her, Donough urged his troops; *"never heed ye the daft thing's rambling prophecy"* and they marched on. Other sources tell us it was the cry of the banshee and the sight of her washing the blood-stained shrouds for the O'Briens that met the troops by the lakeside. The battle with the enemy (led by Diarmait O'Brien, leader of another sept of the O'Brien family) was long and bloody with heavy losses and many wounded. Donough along with his closest kinsmen were among those killed.

The dead, on both sides, including Normans under De Clare, were taken to the abbey for burial. Rory McGrath, (the O'Brian ollamh and chief poet), was in charge, stipulating, as the floors of the abbey ran red with the blood of those killed, who was to be buried where. The O'Brien dead, unsurprisingly were given pride of place:

"For Donough a permanent and worthy tomb, a statelier than for his noble brethren Brien and Murtough and Teigue More. At the prince's side have Brien of Berra laid, in lasting token of your victory; Murtough's grand bulk, beside the stripling (young fellow); by him again, Teigue of Limerick; next in order be Turlough mac Teigue also set."

For the other families he stipulated:

"For the O'Kennedys, have a litter strewn; a cold lair for the O'Hogans, dressed and polished stones planted over the O'Shanachans. Let habitations be prepared for the O'Ahiarns, and narrow flags

*laid over clan-Gillamochanna; a limestone flag, true to rule, over
O'Flaherty. Have O'Donnagan put down in a good place and, as
by you heretofore these members of [your] highborn kindreds have
been extinguished in the mighty battle, even so make ye now ready
and adorn their beds. Over their kerne (the foot soldiers) to be laid
in one long trench be the earth heaped rampart wise: to their English
allies be decent burial given."*

The carnage, graphically described, showed heavy losses
on both sides, among the tribes of Thomond and Connaught; the O'Kennedys, O' Hogans, O' Shanachans,
O'Ahiarns, O'Flahertys and O'Donnagan. So much so that
neither side could claim victory.

*"There were fathers that in their debility with slow and faltering
steps carried their sons, or again sons that bore their fathers, to their
abiding-places of clayey mould; so that with excess of newmade
graves the abbey's earthen floor and the graveyard's area of rest grew
red."*

This story, more than any other, dispels the concept of a
monastic community isolated in a place of peace, dedicated
to prayer and cut off from the rest of 14th century society. If
the time ever existed, it had passed.

Pre Dissolution

The golden days of the Cistercians were probably over by
the mid 14th century. This coincided with the period when
the Black Death swept through Europe radically reducing
the population of towns and cities. As numbers dwindled
the Cistercian hierarchy began to relax some of their strict
rules around austerity, manual labour, and diet. The monks,
long renowned for their farming and fishing expertise, could
no longer afford an army of lay monks (the Conversii), to
do the manual labour and moved into the role of landlord
and rent collector. The monks of Corcomroe, like

Cistercians situated in other remote areas, would have been somewhat protected from the effects of the Black Death but quickly adapted to the new more relaxed rules. The lands, all around Abbey Hill and Bellharbour which the O'Briens had granted in the 12th/13th century to the Cistercians remained abbey lands, but the records show that the abbot of Corcomroe granted the lands of Leath North and South and Gortaclare to the O'Cahans who became the abbey stewards. The O'Cahans were a clerical family and the branch that ended up in Corcomroe were from Derry where the family were influential in other monastic communities including the Cistercians at Lough Swilly.

The Burren records show the O'Cahans had many roles in the local church including Denis O'Cahan who was made bishop of Kilfenora in 1416. Following the O'Cahans, the Tierneys were another influential family associated with Corcomroe, retaining many of the titles and passing on the clerical positions from father to son. It is reported that John Tierney abbot of Corcomroe was made bishop of Kilmacduagh in 1418. Another Cistercian who was also an O'Tierney and abbot of the cell of Corcomroe at Kilshanny became bishop of Kilfenora in 1415.

Abbey and Oughtmama were separated into two discrete parishes sometime between the 14th and 15th centuries. Changes in the construction of Corcomroe Abbey in the 15th century may have been made to accommodate its new role as a parish church. The nave was shortened, and a wall was inserted over which a bell tower was constructed. The changes made were mirrored in a number of other Cistercian abbeys and coincided with a relaxation in the rules whereby the laity were now allowed inside the abbeys. Plenary indulgences were granted to those who contributed to the rebuilding funds, ensuring the forgiveness of their sins. The church building spree came to an end with the dissolution of the monasteries in 1534. Following the dissolution,

Corcomroe Abbey and its lands passed into the hands of Murrough O'Brien.

A parliament in Ireland in 1541 proclaimed Henry VIII King of Ireland and declared it high treason to oppose his title or royal authority. Murrough O'Brien was one of the first to align himself with Henry in his fight against Rome. He did it on the proviso that his Thomond estates were confirmed to him. Henry gave him the title Earl of Thomond. In return Murrough agreed to abandon his native titles and follow English law, dress and ways and pledged allegiance to the English crown. He renounced the Catholic Church and converted to Protestantism. Soon after his assumption of the rank of an English earl, Murrough divided his County Clare estates amongst his sons. His third son Donough (died 1582) inherited Leamanegh and Dromoland and other territories including the lands and abbey of Corcomroe.

While the lands were now back in the hands of the descendant of the original founder, there is no evidence to show when the monks left the abbey. The Cistercian records show that throughout the early 17th century the General Chapter at Citeaux continued to appoint abbots to their Irish abbeys, expecting them to make the annual visits to France even though most of the Irish abbeys were deserted or in ruins at this stage. In many cases the role of the abbot was in name only. In 1628 John O'Dea, a monk of the college at Salamanca, was appointed abbot of Corcomroe. He was the last cleric associated with Corcomroe.

Red Hugh O'Donnell

At the end of the 16th century Corcomroe was again at the centre of conflicts between the O'Brien's and their enemies. The 4th Earl of Thomond, grandson of Murrough O'Brien, fought on the side of Elizabeth I against the Ulster chieftains in the 9 Years War. In revenge Red Hugh O'Donnell (who together with Hugh O Neill led the Ulster rebellion), plundered Clare in 1599. He returned in 1600 to complete the destruction. Passing through the Burren, he encountered O'Maol, formerly chief poet of the O'Briens, whose cattle O'Donnell's men had stolen. In the hope of getting his cattle back, O'Maol composed an elegy flattering Red Hugh. The elegy told that Colmcille had prophesied that O'Donnell would come to Magh Adhair (the ancient inauguration site of the Dal Cais, ancestors to O'Brian kings which was situated near Quin in Co. Clare). His journey would be in revenge for the 11th century destruction of Grianan Aileach, (the ancient fort and ancestral inauguration site of the kings of Ulster), by Murrough O Brian (descendant of the Dalcassians).

> *"From henceforth till final doom the Dalcassians shall not possess Erin. He who will avenge my Aileach, Hugh Oge of steeds of rough roads. The polished body, fame without deceit, the. long hair in ringlets. He is the clamorous Hugh to whom the lords of Tara shall give pledges."*

The feud that O'Maol spoke went back to the 9th century when it was said that warrior Ulstermen invaded the territory near the Shannon River taking back oak timbers from the woods of Cratloe to roof the palace of Grianan Aileach. Two hundred years later, in the 11th century, Murrough O Brien (grandfather of Donal Mor founder of Corcomroe Abbey), instructed his men, following a raid in Ulster and the ransacking of Grianan Aileach, to each bring back a stone from the royal fort. These stones were used in the construction of St Mary's Abbey in Limerick. St Mary's was the site and still is of the tomb of Donal Mor.

O'Maol's elegy and flattery had the desired effect, and his cattle were returned to him and that night, his last night in Thomond according to the annals, Red Hugh camped at Corcomroe Abbey. In the morning, before he left for

Connaught, he ordered the wasting of the district including all the crops and flocks and burning every house and monastery that stood in the way. The devastation was such that all the country was enveloped in smoke and as his men rode through Corcaigh na Cleirigh they were barely able to find their way through the thick smoke arising from the burning countryside left in their wake. Red Hugh didn't get his stones back, but was the burning of Corcomroe Abbey, burial site of the O'Brien kings, the last act of revenge for Grianan Aileach in the centuries old feud?

Post Reformation

When Corcomroe Abbey was abandoned by the monks, it became a home for the dead. A free for all, although not quite, since the wealthy and influential families still took the best positions in the sacred site for their dead and the salvation of their souls. The O'Hehirs requisitioned the north chapel as their family tomb, The O'Hynes's took the sacristy and later in the 19th century the Skerretts built a large tomb and memorial for their family outside the presbytery. But pride of place where the altar would have once stood, the O'Loughlin's built a memorial tomb, inscribed "King of the Burren". The O'Loughlin, descendants of Corco Modruadh from the same family lineage as the O'Connors, had ruled the part of what was originally known as East Corcomroe and later became the lords of the Burren from the 12th/13th century. By the time their tomb was built in the abbey, following the anglicisation of their overlord (Murrough O'Brien the Earl of Thomond), in the 16th century and later the Cromwellian Wars, the O'Loughlin's powers were waning. One has only to look at the names on the gravestones in the presbytery and nave today and notice that most of those relate to families from Munnia, Rossalia and Liagh, areas which historically have been part of Abbey lands dating back to the foundation of the monastery.

19th Century Antiquarians

In the 19th century several antiquarians, including O'Donovan, T.L. Cooke, Fitzgerald, and Westropp visited Corcomroe Abbey and tried to pierce together its long and complicated history. The antiquarian T.L. Cooke visited in the 1830's and left what is one of the earliest surviving drawings of the abbey, including the two-storey gate house which was blown down during a wind in 1839 (shortly after his departure). The antiquarians came to pick over the bones, literally as well as figuratively in the case of William King in 1864, On his visit King took away a 500-year-old skull (from the Battle of Corcomroe?) which is still today preserved in the craniology collection in Trinity College Dublin.

The papers in 1845 wrote of the welcome and acclaim for another member of the O'Brien family to New Quay and Corcomroe Abbey, burial site of his ancestors. The visitor was William Smith O'Brien, MP, nationalist leader, and descendant of the kings of Thomond.

"Cork Examiner - *Friday 12 September 1845*

"WM. SMITH O'BRIEN. ESQ. M. P. This distinguished patriot arrived at New-quay, from the Islands of Arran, about 4 o'clock on Friday last, and shortly after landing proceeded to the residence of Mr. Hynes, of the New-Quay where he was hospitably entertained for the night. In the evening the learned gentleman went to see the celebrated tomb of his ancestor, "Cruhure na Sudarna" (Connor O'Brien), to the Abbey Corcomroe, and before he again reached New-Quay, the whole country was one sheet of flame. Torches blazed on every hill; not a house in the vicinity that was not brilliantly illuminated, and a "monster" bonfire was lighted in front of Mr. Hynes' house; when the lads and lasses of all the villages

around with their musical bands and joyous faces, assembled to tes-
tify their gratitude to him on whom they look as the second great
Captain in their country's struggles for national regeneration."

William Smith O'Brien, brother of Lucius O'Brien (MP for Clare) was an ardent supporter of Catholic Emancipation, the Repeal Movement and fought for independence for Ireland. But after attempts in 1848 at an armed rising in Tipperary failed, he was forced to go on the run, and it was reported in the papers he was trying to make his way to New Quay (where a boat awaited to take him abroad), when he was captured. Found guilty of treason, he was sentenced to be hanged, this was later commuted to transportation to Van Diemens Land.

Dreaming of The Bones

The allure and mystery of Corcomroe Abbey continued to fascinate and in 1919 W. B. Yeats based the play "Dreaming of the Bones" at the abbey. The play recounts the wanderings of a wounded rebel from the 1916 Rising in Dublin. On the run from the authorities, he stumbles at dawn through the ruins of Corcomroe Abbey waiting for a boat to come ashore at Muckinish to help him escape. In the abbey he encounters the ghosts of the King of Thomond and the lovers Diarmuid Mac Murchada and Dervoghilla. The lovers "having sinned after a monstrous fashion" are consumed by remorse. (Their sin or at least Diarmuid's alleged sin was for inviting the Normans Strongbow to Ireland, to assist him in the restoration of his territories.) But they are condemned to remain restless, for 700 years, their lips never meeting as the memories of their crime flow up between them, their ghostly presences haunting Corcomroe Abbey. They ask for forgiveness for their part in first inviting the English to invade Ireland from the young rebel soldier, so that their souls can finally be at rest. When the play was first written during the political upheavals after 1916 it was regarded as too incendiary to be performed and it wasn't until 1931 that it was first staged.

Today

Anyone wandering around Corcomroe Abbey today will be struck by the sense of peace and tranquillity where the building, landscape, light and air conspire to create the feeling that it is truly a sacred place. In the lyrics of Chris Droney from his song "Peaceful Corcomroe".

> *"There's a Sacred place beneath the Burren Mountains where Cistercians came and preached long long ago.*
> *Tis the resting place where lay our forefathers in the lonely graves of Peaceful Corcomroe."*

16. Internal view of the chancel of Corcomroe Abbey

17. External view of Corcomroe Abbey

18. Drawing of the former Corcomroe Abbey Gatehouse by TL Cooke in the 1830's (By kind permission of County Clare Library.)

19. Corcomroe Abbey 12th century effigy of Conaire Siudaine O Brien

10. The Tale of Oughtmama Monastery

Life of Saint Colman Mac Duagh

Beneath Turlough Hill lies the valley of Oughtmama, and in the valley, tucked away, almost out of sight, are the remains of a medieval monastic site dedicated to the 7th century saint, Colman Mac Duagh. Ask anybody locally and they will tell you it's the site of the seven churches, although there are in fact just three churches, in various degrees of preservation. The church remains standing today are not as impressive as neighbouring Corcomroe Abbey, but the monastery at Oughtmama was a beacon for Christians, a place revered, for hundreds of years before the Cistercians came to Corcomroe. The story of Oughtmama, begins with Colman Mc Duagh.

Like many of the regional kings and chieftains of the time, the tribe of Aidne, members of the Ui Faghaidh, rulers of Connaught lay claim to their own saint, a kinsman, Colman McDuagh. Legend has it he was son of Duagh, who ruled over the lands that constitute the present-day diocese of Kilmacduagh. The story goes that the jealous father,

Duagh, tried to have his pregnant wife Rhinagh drowned in the river when she made a prophesy that her unborn son would grow up to be the most powerful member of his royal lineage. Miraculously Rhinagh survived the attempt on her life: rescued by the angels, she was washed up at Kiltartan, where the marks of the rope that had been put around her neck are said to be still visible on a rock. When her son Colman was born (around 560 AD), fearing that his life would be short-lived, Rhinagh, asked two passing clerics (one blind and one deaf) to baptize him. In the absence of water, the clerics, rubbed the earth beneath the tree, where the mother was sheltering, and a fountain sprang up. Having baptized Colman, they then rubbed their eyes and ears with the water from the spring and the sight and hearing of the clerics were restored. Rhinagh handed over the child to the monks for safekeeping and they took the baby with them when they returned to their monastery on Inis Mor in the Aran Islands.

St. Colman grew up on Inis Mor in the monastery of St Enda and became a monk. He founded a monastery at Kilmurvey on Inis More at the end of the 6th century before deciding to leave the communal life to become a hermit. Following in the footsteps of the desert fathers he took himself away to a lonely place, in this case the Burren. The description of his hermit's existence is captured beautifully in the 19th century poem by Mary E Connolly.

Colman Mac Duagh in the Burren

*"Here steel-grey mountains proudly rear their heads and seem to
    touch the ever-varying skies.*
Where once but Burren's eagles' cries were heard,
And sea-fowl's mew, and lap-wing's plaintive walt.
*Where the deep silences were never stirred by human accents, frivo-
    lous or grave;*
Here Saint McDuagh came from Aranmore.
Came from that ancient isle of saint and sage.
His soul a thirst for that great solitude,
That life apart from earth and things of earth,
That close communion with Eternal Truth.
*And here for seven years that quickly sped on lightning wings of
    ecstasy and prayer,*
Alone with God, 'twixt earth and heav'n, he dwelt.
*His bed-the hard unyielding mountain rock; His food-what bird
    and beast brought unto him,*
And herbs and berries gathered in the glen;
*His thirst he quenched with water from yon fount Yon crystal fount-
    and, drinking, made it blessed.*
And like the mist that rises with the sun
At break of day, and melts into the air,
His prayers arose from morn to even-song,
And still again from eve to matin-hour,
Arose and mingled with the angels' praise,
*Around the throne, the great white throne of God. And here, per-
    haps, he knelt, this rock upon,*
*And held sweet converse with the great All- High; And there, be-
    neath that beetling mountain crest,*
*It may be that he met his kinsman Columba, Iona's dove-and spoke
    and prayed with him.*
*O thrice-blest rock! O mountain sanctified By Columba's prayers,
    and Colman's ecstasies! O Burren bare and desolate and lone,*
Great is the honour God has done to thee!"

Legend says he lived in a cave, enduring long periods of fasting and praying in an isolated wooded valley in the townland of Kilhilla where he was visited by St Columba. Today most of the trees have gone, replaced with bare limestone. On the side of the hill, you can still see the cave, holy well and ruins of a tiny oratory and even today, over 1500 years later it's a lonely place and could serve as a place of sanctuary for someone seeking solitude at the edge of the world.

Colman lived here for 7 years and 40 days with just a manservant for occasional company. On Easter Sunday, after forty days of a Lenten fast, he prayed to God to provide food for his hungry manservant. Meanwhile in Durcas fort in Kinvara, (the ruins of which lie close by Dunguaire Castle), about five miles away, his kinsman Guaire was sitting down to a feast. Suddenly the food and dishes, on the wings of angels, were carried out the window towards the place where Colman was praying. When the food arrived at the mouth of Colman's cave, the manservant, overcome by his hunger, gorged himself to death, literally! The site where he is buried is still known today as the "Grave of the Saint's Servant.' Guaire, with his soldiers on horseback, followed the dishes, along the road still called 'Bothar Na Miosa" (Road of the Dishes). On arriving at the cave and finding his cousin kneeling in prayer, Guaire, impressed by the faith of his cousin, entreated St Colman to set up a monastery and become the bishop in charge of the Aidne territory. Colman reluctantly, abandoned his hermitage and built a church and monastery at the place now called Kilmacduagh (translated church of Mac Duagh) where he ruled as abbot and bishop for many years. Later in life, Colman, his soul again having *a thirst for that great solitude,'* left Kilmacduagh and moved back to his hermetic existence, this time settling in Oughtmama.

His death is recorded as occurring at Oughtmama in 632 A.D., but his body was afterwards taken to Kilmacduagh. A small mortuary chapel existed up until the 18th century in Kilmacduagh which marked the site of his burial, known as Leaba Mac Duagh (Mac Duagh's bed). Kilmacduagh was a beacon for pilgrims visiting the shrine of St Colman for hundreds of years. It appeared that where Colman went, others soon followed and Oughtmama (translated as ucht máma, meaning "breast of a yoke", i.e., the upper front of a mountain pass), also became the site of a monastery.

Today at Oughtmama, besides the ruins of three churches, the site includes evidence of a monastic enclosure, which marked out the areas reserved for the monks and those accessible to lay members. The scant archaeological and documentary evidence available points to Oughtmama as being an important religious centre from the early medieval period and it appears to have stayed in use up until the 16th/17th century.

Early History Up Until the 12th Century

Prior to the 11th century most churches in Ireland were made from wood, which could explain why such little evidence exists of the earliest churches at Oughtmama. Sinead Ni Ghabhlain in her research into parish formation and churches of Kilfenora Diocese, dated the Oughtmama stone churches according to the style of masonry in the stonework. The Western church, the largest, was the earliest stone church and it has been dated to the 10th or 11th century. It's probable that this was built on a pre-existing wooden church site. The second and third churches were built slightly later.

The 'Leabhar Breac', (written in the 15th century, but referring to saints and religious texts from the period up to the 7th and 8th centuries AD), references the three Saint Colmans of Uchtmama, as; Colman, son of Lugaid, son of Loegaire, son of Nial of the Nine Hostages; Colman, son of Lugaid, son of Ængus, son of Naitfraich, son of Corc, son of Lugaid;

Colman, son of Lugaid, son of Conall, son of Brian, son of Eochaid Muidmedon. The race of "Lugaid" were legendary kings of Ireland with claims to the kingdom of Munster. While the historical evidence for this early period is sparse, there are indications that part of the barony of the Burren came under the rule of the Ui Fiachrach Aidhne, the rulers of south Connaught, during the first centuries of the first millennium but later from the 7th/8th century the Dal Cais pushed north and became overlords of the Corco Modruadh, the rulers of Corcomroe and the Burren (which was one territory until the 12th/13th century). Before the advent of Christianity in Ireland, each tribe had their own local gods which linked them to their territories, and in the first centuries after St Patrick, it was common for tribes to lay claim and ancestral links with saints as it confirmed their title and legitimated sacred rights to their lands. While Colman Mac Duagh was saint for the Ui Fachraich Aidne, he was also their kinsman. It's possible that with the rise of the Dal Cais (the original tribe of the O' Brien's) from the 8th century to become kings of Munster and Thomond they paid homage to their own saints of Munster ancestry. The new patron saints of Oughtmama, the Munster Colmans, would be regarded as the kinsmen of the ruling dynasty.

In 1893 Frost, an historian, wrote that repairs undertaken in Oughtmama, by the Office of Public Works found early medieval Stone Cross Slabs and crosses, which appeared to cover tombs in the floor of largest church. Westropp, a late 19th /early 20th century archaeologist, also refers to these stone slabs with early Christian inscriptions, when he visited in the 1900's. These types of slabs, found in many early monastic sites, can usually be dated to the first millennium AD. However, these have since disappeared and can no longer throw any light on who, if anyone, is buried there, or if they marked the graves of the three Colmans or early abbots.

Colman was a very common name for Irish saints in the first millennium. In the Martyrology of Donegal there are 98 St Colmans. The Martyrology is a list of all the Irish Saints, written in the 17th century by Michael O'Cleirigh and based on a series of earlier documents from 8th century with biographical notes of Irish saints. The name Colman was seen as the diminutive of Colm, which is the Irish for dove and in Christianity the dove is symbolic of God's spirit, which probably explains why so many holy men would have chosen or have been given the name Colman.

Prior to the 12th century the canonisation process i.e., declaring someone a saint, was managed by the local bishops and abbots. The process involved an inquiry into the sanctity of the person's life and the miracles attributed to that person's intercession. When the canonisation was approved, it was commonplace to set up an altar over the saint's tomb and transfer his relics to a church. This explains the proliferation of Irish saints from the early centuries after Saint Patrick and is probably also an indication of the influence of the secular rulers in the canonisation process. It could explain why so many saints were kinsmen of the local chieftains and kings. After the 12th century, and with the greater control of Rome over the Irish church, the process of canonisation became more formal and required papal review and approval.

References to Oughtmama in early historical documents include the 'Litany of Aengus', written in the 8 or 9th century. This tract was a listing of Irish Saints and the practice of pilgrimage. The litany invokes the seven bishops of Oughtmama. J. Fahy in his history of the Kilmacduagh Diocese written in 1905, has suggested that the seven bishops may have fled from Kilmacduagh following raids by the Vikings and could have sought temporary refuge at Oughtmama. However, Oughtmama was not immune as the Annals of the FourMasters state that Norsemen raided Oughtmama in

749 and 820 AD whilst on their rampages along the west coast of Ireland. History shows that the Vikings targeted monasteries, at a time when much of the wealth in the country, in form of silver and gold and other precious metals, was held by the church.

Oughtmama has many of the characteristics found in early medieval monastic sites. Its entrance is marked with a leacht, or stone altar found close to the churches. This was probably the base of a cross originally. Crosses were common near entrances to early medieval monastic sites, signifying that the visitor was entering a place of sanctuary. The main church and the second church are contained in the inner enclosure, whilst the third is in the middle enclosure. The inner enclosure, regarded as the holy of holies, usually contained the monks' church. Additional chapels usually were set aside as shrines or for women and or other lay members to worship. It's possible that the third church at Oughtmama was a shrine chapel set aside to hold relics.

The early Irish monasteries were usually protected and supported by the patronage of the local chieftain and benefactor, but the monks were also farmers and crafts people. The outer enclosure at Oughtmama is half in the rich tillage soil and half in the rough limestone typical of the Burren. This provided land for tillage but also winter feed for cattle and animal grazing. Near Oughtmama there is evidence that a local stream was diverted, and a horizontal mill was in use. While the mill and the stream were in the lands of the monks of Oughtmama, the hydraulic expertise of diverting streams and rivers, bears all the hallmarks of the Cistercians. The horizontal mill, if dated to the early medieval period, was a major advancement in corn grinding and would have allowed the monks to gain a lucrative income from local people for its use.

Period from the 12th Century

In the 12th century several events happened which would have had an impact on the lives of the monks in Oughtmama. The first of these related to the reform of the church. The historical references show that the church in Rome was concerned that the Irish church was too autonomous and not abiding by the dictates or doctrines of the church in Rome. There were also concerns and belief that it was corrupt; lack of priestly celibacy was one such concern. The reality appeared to be that local control was in the hands of the monastic abbots and Rome sought to bring it under its influence and in line with rest of Europe. Instigated by Malachy, Archbishop of Armagh, changes were agreed at a number of synods; Rathbasil in 1111, Kells in 1152 and Tuam in 1154. A new hierarchical structure was set up consisting of archdioceses, dioceses, and parishes. For Oughtmama this meant that in 1210 the Council of Tuam transferred ownership of the church lands from the abbots and the hereditary stewards to the local bishop. Oughtmama now came within the new diocese of Kilfenora and while the hereditary keepers still ran the monastery, they were now tenants of the bishop. As part of this reform Oughtmama became a parish, with its own parish church, priest, tithes, and endowment, under the control of the bishop of Kilfenora. The Western church at Oughtmama appears to have been enlarged for reuse as a parish church and the two smaller stone churches were built during the last quarter of the twelfth and early decades of the thirteenth century, probably replacing earlier wooden churches on the same sites.

The archaeological evidence from Sinead Ni Ghabhlain shows that several churches in the new diocese of Kilfenora were built in this period, many in a style unique to north Clare and south Galway, suggesting that the same masons were used in their construction. In Ireland with the replacement of abbots by bishops as church leaders, it became the norm for the territorial power structure previously based around the old monasteries to shift. Many of the old monasteries disappeared as they had no part to play in the new reformed church hierarchy. Oughtmama, like many of the other monastic sites in the Burren, appears to have weathered the change, making the transition to parish church, and retaining its church lands. One possibility is that the local chieftains, Corcu McDruadh, and later their descendants, the O'Loughlin's and O'Connors, still retained their influence and control in the new diocese and the retention of the old structure with the church centred around the old monastery site, suited their purposes, and so ensured their continued authority in religious as well as secular matters.

The Anglo-Norman invasion of Ireland in the 12th century was a major event for the Irish church. Oughtmama, situated in the North of Clare, remained relatively unscathed and continued under Gaelic rule throughout this period. The third and final event was the foundation of the Cistercian Abbey of Corcomroe Abbey, less than a half a mile from the site of Oughtmama churches. The founder of the abbey is thought to be either Donal Mor O'Brien, or his son Donough Cairbreach and is dated to the end of 12th or very early 13th century. As they did in many parts of Ireland it's likely that the first Cistercians settled in Oughtmama before building their abbey and moving to the current site. The O'Brien's, who were already the overlords of the Burren and now the benefactors of Corcomroe Abbey, handed over a large part of the lands of Oughtmama to the new abbey. This became Abbey parish in the 13th century, separate from Oughtmama. It appears that what was previously one territory or Tuatha, now became two parishes. Half of the patronage and tithes, which would have gone to Oughtmama, was now given to Corcomroe Abbey. The organization of the townlands of Oughtmama and Abbey seems to have been decided to ensure each had access to the coast as well as good lands, but also some mountainous areas for grazing. While today it is one parish, the electoral divisions of the townlands split between Abbey and Oughtmama has survived almost one thousand years later.

However, despite losing half its land and being controlled by the bishop of Kilfenora, Oughtmama monastery appears to have continued to flourish. This was the period when the new churches were built, and the parish church extended. In contrast, the abbey of Corcomroe seems to have become poorer in the following centuries. Records show that in the 15th century Abbey and Oughtmama shared a single vicar or priest. Like many other monasteries, which had lost large parts of their income to the diocesan bishops after the church reforms Oughtmama too would have turned to pilgrimages as a means of support.

Place of Pilgrimage

From the 12th century in Europe, pilgrimages became the primary occupation of many church sites, with pilgrims flocking to sacred sites, to venerate the relics, bones, blood, or items of clothing of the saints and to holy wells and sacred trees for cures for body and soul. Looking at the Burren today one can still see the footpaths through the mountains, where the pilgrims would have trod. Temple Cronan in Carran was a well-known pilgrim site where the 7th century stone tent shaped shrine next to the church is believed to have contained the bones of Saint Cronan. Kilmacduagh, as well as being the burial site of St Colman MacDuagh, also had his crozier. The crozier, while now stored in the National Museum in Dublin, had been held by the hereditary keepers up until the 19th century. For those who venerated Saint Colman, both Oughtmama and Teamphall Mac Duagh in the

Aran Islands would also have been important centres for pilgrims.

In the 16th century Pope Paul V created a pilgrim route of seven churches in Rome, stipulating that the pilgrim who visited and prayed at each one of the seven would be granted a plenary indulgence, saving a soul from Purgatory. The site of Oughtmama is still known today as the seven churches. There are no indications that seven churches ever existed there, but this seems to be a common occurrence, with Clonmacnoise, Kilmacduagh, Na Seacht Teamphall of Inis More and Glendalough and many more monasteries, all having the title seven churches associated with them. The explanation is that each site had seven altars or penitential stations including holy wells. Prayers at each of the seven would qualify the pilgrim for the plenary indulgence. The prayers of the pilgrim were regarded as being more powerful if their visit coincided with the feast day of the saint of the founding church or well. For Oughtmama the tradition has been to visit the holy well on the 14th of November, a day historically which the people of Oughtmama declared a holiday from work.

In the Martyrology of Donegal (transcribed from documents of the 8th or 9th centuries) Colman Mac Duagh appears to be listed twice, once as Colman of the Hy Fachraigh and once as Colman Bishop of Kilmacduagh. The first one has a feast day of 27th October and the second 3rd February. At Kilmacduagh, the tradition has been to celebrate St Colman's feast day on the 29th of October but in the oratory and cave at Kilhilla the custom has been for a pattern to take place on the 3rd of February. A pattern would have involved visiting the well and probably each of the churches and the leacht in a predefined order and praying at each. Up until the mid-19th century the pattern day on the feast of the founding saint included celebrations, singing and dancing but from the mid 19th century, such celebrations were frowned on by an increasing puritanical church and the practice of holding a pattern was discontinued in many places.

In Oughtmama the well of Saint Colman has always attracted visitors as it is traditionally associated with a cure for eyes. There is also a large cut "C" shaped stone on the ground near the western church. It is said that if you place your head underneath the stone, your headaches will be cured. The stone appears to have fallen or been moved from the head of the original east window.

Later History

It appears from the evidence that Oughtmama continued as a parish church and possibly pilgrim site until the middle of the 17th century. The Clerical Registry for the priests of Oughtmama during the 15th century shows the same surnames repeated (for instance O 'Gowan and Nestor) suggesting that religious control was concentrated in a small number of families who had influence to decide who would be priest and kept the role in their family.

First the reformation and later the penal laws, had a devastating effect on the Catholic church and pilgrimage traditions in Ireland. It's likely that the churches at Oughtmama were abandoned and fell into decay by the end of the 17th century. Under the penal laws a decree was issued that all parish priests were required to be registered on a central registry from 1700 and pay two sureties of £50. The parish priest register at Ennis for 1704 shows Walter Markham then aged 44 as the parish priest for the parish of Abbey and Oughtmama since 1687 and in 1704 he was resident in the townland of Turlough. In a poem from the 17th century about the O'Loughlins of the Burren attributed by O'Rahilly to one of the O'Dalaigh poets, a mention is made of Markham renting an O'Loughlin castle which may have been the one based in Turlough. In the report for the state of popery in 1731, there is no priest identified for the parish of Abbey and Oughtmama.

Today

Today, Oughtmama monastery is an enigmatic place, as the hazel scrub and bushes at the foot of Turlough Hill encroach on the monastic site. The most obvious landmarks are the first two churches, the largest church, which is considered to have been the parish church, and a smaller church next to it. Both churches are aligned east to west, which is common with most church buildings, with the altar facing east, based on the biblical reference: "For as lightning that comes from the east is visible even in the west, so will be the coming of the Son of Man."

The third church, standing a little distance away is certainly the most intriguing. It is in a poor state of repair with just one full wall of the church still standing. Its layout with the doorway on the south wall and the orientation southwest to northeast, is an exception to the design and alignment of most churches. One theory is that churches which were designed to hold relics or commemorate saints were often aligned to face the rising sun on the feast day of the founding saint. Its orientation, facing south, is identical to that of St Benan's Oratory on Inis Mor, one of the smallest and oldest churches in Ireland, regarded by many as the tomb shrine of St Benan. Tomb shrines were designed to hold the remains or relics of the saint and were a place of pilgrimage. St Benan was a disciple of St Patrick and was sent by him to preach the gospel and convert those that St Patrick didn't get around to. The Tripartite of St Patrick states that St Benan was sent to convert the Corco Modruadh in North Thomond to Christianity. In the 5th/6th century the Aran Islands were part of the territory of the Corco Modruadh and St Benan's feast day is 6th of November, which is very close

29th October the feast day of St Colman celebrated in Kilmacduagh.

Whoever the three Munster St Colmans once revered at Oughtmama were has been long forgotten and only the story of Saint Colman Mac Duagh, the reluctant bishop, who still captures the imagination, survives. While Saint Colman Mac Duagh is reputed to have died at Oughtmama and his body taken to Kilmacduagh, maybe some remnant of him was preserved at Oughtmama and that the site of his hermitage where he played out his final days was at, or close by, the site of this third church. A church where a thin, beautifully designed, slit window on the remaining standing wall lets the sun shine through to the hallowed ground where St Colman, his relics or remains once lay and where he spent his last days:

His soul a thirst for that great solitude,
That life apart from earth and things of earth,
That close communion with Eternal Truth.

20. Map of Abbey and Oughtmama townlands. (By kind permission of County Clare Library)

21. Stone also known as a stoup outside the western church at Oughtmama

22. View of Oughtmama churches1 and 2

23. View of Oughtmama church 3

11. The Tale of Saint Patrick's Well

St Patrick's Well

Tradition has it that of all the counties in Ireland, Clare was the one that St Patrick never visited. Instead, he is said to have knelt on a hill; Mount Fintine on the Limerick side of the Shannon, with a view of Clare that stretched to the western shores and blessed what was then Thomond. The hill, until the early 20th century, was said to have a flagstone on the top with the imprint of St Patrick's knees. The Clare tradition has it that one of the reasons why he never visited is that when he arrived on these shores, County Clare was already Christian!

Yet at the top of the Corker Hill, along the Green Road, an unpaved road which skirts the front of Abbey Hill, a stile leads to the site of St Patrick's Well. The well, dedicated to Saint Patrick, is said to have been blessed by him in the 5th century. The well is in the townland of Rosalia, which straddles the Clare Galway border and which, in the 5th century, was possibly part of Connaught and not Thomond. In the choice of a site for a sacred well, you would have difficulty finding one with a more impressive view. Lying to the south-east of Abbey Hill, the views of Currenrue, Doorus, Aughinish and Galway Bay stretching into the distance are breath taking.

A spring flows from the cliff face into the sunken stone lined well, where people have placed offerings of photos, statues, and mementos. The waters, having been blessed by St Patrick, are said to have healing powers, particularly for ailments of the limbs. As children, we, like many over the centuries, climbed from the bottom of Abbey Hill to visit the well on the 17th of March, Saint Patrick's Day. As well as paying homage to the patron saint, the belief was that the curative powers of the waters were stronger on the saint's feast day. Holy wells were the site of Christian baptisms until the Irish church came under Roman influence, when baptismal fonts were placed inside churches. Many of the early Christian churches were built close by wells for this purpose.

A hawthorn tree stands just a few yards from St Patrick's well, with bits of cloths, hankies and ribbons hanging from the branches. In pagan times those seeking purification or cures would dip a strip of cloth (called a "clootie") in the well, then apply it to the affected body part, before hanging the cloth on the nearby Hawthorn tree. The belief was that by the time the sun had bleached the cloth and the passage of time had cleaned it, the part of the body it had touched would be cured. The Hawthorn tree blooms in May, so the expression "don't change a clout until May is out" refers to leaving the cloth on the tree, until the sun has bleached it, by which time the body should be healed. The tradition continues in Christian times, as the sacred springs bring healing through a belief in prayers to the saint of the well. In his "Autumnal Rambles Around New Quay" in the 1840's T.L. Cooke describes the purity of the water from St Patrick's well, gushing forth from the cliff and a common belief among the locals that water from the well would never boil if heated near the vicinity of the well.

On the other side of Abbey Hill, in the vicinity of Corcomroe Abbey, there exists another well, Tober Sheila. In Irish myths Sheila was the wife of Saint Patrick and had a feast day on 18th of March. Sheila was seen as a representation or symbol of Irish womanhood and up until the mid-19th century the festivals for St Patricks Day extended to St Sheila's Day. Sheila Na Gig, represented as stone carvings in 100s of medieval buildings, embodies the cycle of birth, fertility, and death.

Memorial Leacht

Between the well and the Green Road is a stone square structure known as a Leacht. The leacht at Saint Patrick's well is very similar to some others found at entrances to former ecclesiastical sites in the Burren, for example Balyballan. In many cases these were used as the base for stone crosses and slabs which date from early Christianity. They served as markers on the boundary between secular and holy places, or later as penitential stations. Some are believed to be burial mounds, stone altars, or resting places of coffins on the way to the cemetery. The leacht at St Patrick's Well may have replaced an early Christian base for a cross or a penitential station although it looks as if its use and purpose changed when it was dedicated as a memorial.

Today the inscription on the leacht reads:

LORD JESUS
CHRIST HAVE
MERCY ON
US PRAY FOR
THE SOULES
OF JOHN CORNYN AND HIS
WIFE MARY MCNEMARA 1700

Next to the inscription, etched into stone, is the drawing of a face, today the emblem for Burren Beo. A similar drawing with a happier face is contained among the stones surrounding the well. It is thought that the drawing in the well was previously on the other side of the leacht, or it may be that both stones were originally in the surrounds of the well. Decorative and carved heads are found in many wells, dedicated to the early Celtic Christian saints. The ancient celts saw the head as the source of knowledge and head stones were placed in the well to activate the power of healing.

So, who were John Cornyn and Mary McNamara? It has often been suggested that the stone masons made a mistake, and that John Cornyn should read John Comyn. The Comyn and the McNamara's were prominent Clare families and there are many instances where Comyn and McNamara family members intermarried. However, there is other evidence that supports the view that the name Cornyn was not a mistake. The O'Brien rentals show that Bartholomew McNamara from Doolin rented land at Rosalia, Munnia and Murtyclough in the first half of the 18th century. It's possible that Mary McNamara was a sister or aunt of Bartholomew, hence the connection with Rossalia. The two names John Cornyn and Maria McNamara also appear as the patrons of a silver chalice, now in the National Museum of Ireland. The chalice (often called the McNamara chalice.) is inscribed: *"Orate pro D Joanne Cornin et Maria Macnemarra qui me fieri fecerunt anno Dni 1683"* Translated as: *"Pray for John Cornin and Maria Macnemarra who caused me to be made A.D. 1683".* The name and dates are similar to the name on the monument or the leacht. The surnames Cornin, Cornyn and Corneen are interchangeable.

This chalice is one of many examples of silver chalices inscribed with the names of the patrons, which were made in Galway between the16th and 18th centuries. It also has the initials "BF," for Bartholomew Fallon, a Galway silversmith.

The history and origin of the chalice from the time it was made is unknown. It surfaced in the collection of Robert Day, a Cork collector and antiquarian who purchased it in London in the late 19th century. In 1888 he sold it at Sotheby's in London when it was purchased by Mr N C McNamara of Grosvenor Place London. He in turn sold it at Christies in 1910, when it was purchased for the National Museum of Ireland.

To find out more about the names inscribed on the leacht at Patrick's Well and the chalice, an historian in the 19th century, Mr Dermot Gleeson made enquiries with the sergeant in Ballyvaughan. The only information he gleaned was from a local man called Quin. He confirmed that Cornin, Cornyn or Curneen were not local names but in Penal Times there was a teacher called Cornin who taught locally at Poll na Duirc, (translated as the gloomy, morose, or silent place), a cell, possibly a hermit's cell, in the grounds of Corcomroe and as some kind of penance for a killing he built the memorial at Saint Patrick's Well. It's possible that Cornin was the son or relation of the couple John Cornyn and Mary McNamara whose names are on the leacht and chalice. It is known that many members of the third order of Franciscans became teachers to evade capture following the Penal Laws, so Cornin may have been a friar who built the memorial in honour of his parents. The chalice may have been donated to an abbey or convent until it was forced to close following the implementation of the penal laws against Popery.

The author Mervyn Archdell, in the Hibernius Monastium manuscript (1786) in a listing which includes all Franciscan Friaries in Ireland has a reference to a Friary at the front of what is now Abbey Hill. The reference states: *"Beagh – there was a monastery here of the third order of Franciscan Friars, the abbey of Beaghan in the parish of Abbey County Clare."* It goes on to state *"it was on the north side of Corcomroe Abbey and bounded in the north by Kinvara bay".* Later 19th century antiquarians, including John O'Donovan have refuted the existence of a friary church here. However, in his "Autumnal Rambles around New Quay" T.L. Cooke refers to a stone church at the back of what was then the village of Munnia on the side of the Beha Mountain close by a spring. *"The inhabitants of the place denominate it Temple Liaghagh, in English, the 'Stone Church', and the villagers collect therein for their domestic uses the water which trickles from the mountain's side."* The north side of Abbey Hill, facing Galway Bay was called Beha Hill in the 18th and 19th century (According to T.L. Cooke). It's interesting that the well, referred to by Cooke with the stone church is marked as Tobar Brathaireen, translated as 'the Well of the little brother' or Friar Minor on the 1840s ordnance survey map. The stone church referred to by Cooke may have been a small church (or Mass Chapel as they were sometimes called), of the third order of St Francis used during Penal times when 'strolling friars' wandered the country administering to the flocks in defiance of the authorities. No trace of it exists today.

24. View of Galway Bay from St Patrick's Well

25. The McNamara Chalice preserved in the National Museum in Dublin

12. The Tale of Turlough Hill

Turlough Hill

Corcomroe Abbey, nestling in the foothills of the Burren, is an iconic Christian landmark. It dates back a thousand years to an era when the Cistercian monks left their homes to build a community among the 'fertile rock' and set out a new and authentic way of living in response to the call of God. Less than two kilometers from the abbey, on a mountain top there exists another site, where 3,500 years earlier, (at the same time that Newgrange and before Stonehenge was built), another group of people left their homes to gather, pay homage to and petition their gods. This site sits at the summit of Turlough Hill. The only proof we have of the existence of those people are the remains of huts and enclosures. Nothing whatsoever has been found of the people themselves, not one scrap of bone. We have no evidence if they wore clothes, what they ate, how they protected themselves against the cold winds and rain on the mountain top. We do know that the area around here, in this period, would have been heavily wooded, much of it difficult to traverse and even today it is not an easy place to get to.

What is The Evidence?

So, who were these people and what were the beliefs and purpose that drove them to ascend to the summit of an inaccessible mountain top, build temporary homes and monuments while leaving little trace? Turlough Hill summit is unique in that it is quite level and composed of two summits, east and west, which together with a depression in between looks like a giant footprint from the air. As there is no documentary evidence, archaeologists can only glean from what little remains who these people were and why they chose to build huts on the most exposed summit of a remote mountain.

Through a mixture of field work and aerial photography, Stefan Bergh from NUIG Archaeology Department has examined the evidence that can be construed from the landscape. This showed the remains of over 130 circular huts, which all together could have housed up to 500 people. Many of the huts are linked (semidetached dwellings!) and they are located in small clusters not far from a prehistoric enclosure on one summit and a large stone cairn on the other, which may have been centers for rituals. The positioning of the houses in the east appears to be a mirror image of the position in the west, with the two summits separated by a depression. The bare landscape, open to the winds, the temporary nature of the huts and the lack of evidence of normal domestic everyday activity, such as pens for animals, evidence of waste etc., adds credence to the belief that this was purely a site of ritual and not a place of permanent settlement where people lived year-round, but a place that was reused for short visits possibly over many centuries. The distribution of the huts concentrated on the highest, most exposed parts (the last place you would expect people to set up home!), the location of the cairn and the stone enclosures, all point to a people who had a definite ground plan and knew exactly what they were doing.

The mountain top offers spectacular views to the north-west over Galway Bay, east over South Galway and North-east Clare and south to Slieve Carron which in turn is also dominated by a hilltop cairn. The views from Turlough Hill at the time the huts were in use, would probably have shown a landscape still heavily wooded stretching to the coast. It is probable that the people who gathered here came from the surrounding area, the Burren, and South Galway and prob-ably further afield, with the mountain top becoming a focal point for different tribes. So why did they come, what drove them to put such a huge amount of effort into building the huts and ritual monuments in such an isolated place?

Stone Fort Enclosure

In 1899 Westropp, the antiquarian, visited the site and ex-plored the enclosure on the eastern summit. He described a huge stone fort, the second largest he had encountered in Clare, surrounded by a wall, nine to twelve foot in thickness. A drawing he produced, provides a glimpse of what the fort looked like then before further deterioration over the last hundred years. The enclosure had at least nine and possibly twelve gateways with a natural gully used as the main en-trance. Westropp noted that in all the other prehistoric forts in Clare, there was only one entrance. The purpose of the forts was mainly to defend the inhabitants, which was better managed by having just one entrance. But with at least nine entrances, the enclosure in Turlough clearly wasn't designed to keep people or animals out! So, what could have been the purpose of the gateways? What rituals and ceremonial activ-ities were performed here that involved passing through multiple entrances and exits?

Who Were These People?

From what little we know, the people who came to Turlough Hill would have been early farmers, reliant on the weather to plant their crops in Spring, provide a climate for growth in Summer and fruitful harvest in Autumn. They would have been dependent on the rain falling and the sun shining at the right times. They had an understanding of the cosmos and their place in the world. They were able to read the sky, track the movements of the stars and believed that their invocations to the gods and the inhabitants of another realm, spirits, and ancestors and through their offerings could tap into a well of wisdom to influence the weather and ensure their livelihood.

Why Come to A Mountain Top?

Throughout history there are many places where mountains are venerated as special places, with their close proximity to the sky symbolizing links with otherworld of gods and spirits. The mountain top at Turlough Hill was clearly a special place, a symbolic place where earth and sky met, close to the heavens and the Otherworld while offering views of the territories that the tribes would have claimed as their own and the ocean from Galway Bay over which their ancestors would have travelled. While there is no trace of what rituals they performed at Turlough Hill and no artefacts have been uncovered from the site which would give some clues, the positioning of the cairn, probably a burial chamber for their dead (who were remembered and revered), the enclosure on the summit and another hexagonal stone enclosure to the east would have played a role in those rituals. This place on the mountain top, where the veil between the normal and the supernatural were seen as thinner, would have been endowed with a holiness that remains one of the greatest mysteries of the Burren.

According to Johnson Westropp:

"The footprints of an elder race are here,
And memories of an old heroic time,
And shadows of the old mysterious faith;
So that the place seems haunted, and strange sounds
Float on the wind."

26. View from Turlough Hill looking out over Galway Bay

27. Evidence in the soil of one of the 130 huts identified.

28. Early 20th century drawing by Westropp of the fort on Turlough Hill

Meet the Author

Kathleen Fawle was born and grew up in New Quay where 5 generations of her ancestors have lived and farmed for over 200 years. Kathleen, an amateur historian, has studied History at University College Dublin and Archaeology at the National University of Ireland Galway and at Oxford University. Prior to writing "The History of New Quay in 12 Tales" Kathleen worked as a Financial Business Analyst in the city of London. Today she divides her time between New Quay and Hertfordshire in England where she lives with her husband.

Acknowledgements

In my research I am grateful to the following who helped me along the way, sharing documentation and pointers for further inquiry.

Emma Barrett, great granddaughter of Elizabeth Skerrett for her photos of Finavarra House and original documents relating to the Skerrett family.

Kathleen Villiers Tuthill for her references and copies of documents relating to Alexander Nimmo and the development of New Quay pier in the 1820's.

Sinead Ni Ghabhlain for providing a copy of her unpublished thesis on the history of the churches of Kilfenora including Oughtmama.

The librarians of NLI for assistance in locating and providing copies of documents.

The librarians of the British Library for help in locating old maps.

The University of Essex for access to the online census summaries of the 19th century.

The staff of Clare Library for assistance in locating documents from their archives.

For sharing local tales and answering my questions I am indebted to my family and the people of New Quay including those deceased; my father and uncle Michael and Patrick Fawle and to Mary Madden and P.J. Leenane whose yarns of the old ways kept us children in thrall and sparked my fascination with history.

Joan Frantschuk of Woven Red Author Services for making my book so eye-catching and easy to read.

Finally, thanks to my husband Chris, son Michael and daughter Eva for their continued support and encouragement as well as endless reading and editing with suggestions for revisions and for their patience in humouring me as I dragged them across fields, mountains, and shoreline in my research.

Bibliography

Online Primary Sources

In writing this book I drew on a wide range of sources and particularly on the newspaper archives. The website: https://www.britishnewspaperarchive.co.uk has proved an invaluable fountain of information on contemporary news in the 19th century.

As well as the newspaper archives, my research included a trawl through the following sources online:

Tithe Apportionment Books, 1823- 1837, National Archives of Ireland. Available at http://titheapplotmentbooks.nationalarchives.ie/search/tab/home.jsp

Schools Folklore Collection 1837 – 38 Fiontar (DCU) & National Folklore Collection (UCD). Available at: https://www.duchas.ie/en

Griffith's Valuation, 1848 – 1864. Available at: https://www.askaboutireland.ie/griffith-valuation/

Annals of the Four Masters - Annala Rioghachta Eireann: Annals of the Kingdom of Ireland, by the Four Masters, from the earliest period to the year 1616, translated by O'Donovan, John (2nd ed.), 1856, 7 volumes, Royal Irish Academy:

Volume 1 (2952 BC – AD 902), Dublin, Hodges, Smith, and co., 1856 – via CELT: English, Irish

Volume 2 (AD 903–1171), Dublin, Hodges, Smith, and co., 1856 – via CELT: English, Irish

Volume 3 (AD 1172–1372), Dublin, Hodges, Smith, and co., 1856 – via CELT: English, Irish

Volume 4 (AD 1373–1500), Dublin, Hodges, Smith, and co., 1856 – via CELT: English, Irish

Volume 5 (AD 1501–1588), Dublin, Hodges, Smith, and co., 1856 – via CELT: English, Irish

Volume 6 (AD 1589–1616), Dublin, Hodges, Smith, and co., 1856 – via CELT: English, Irish

Volume 7 (Indices), Dublin, Hodges, Smith, and co., 1856 – via CELT

Annals of Inisfallen: https://celt.ucc.ie/published/T100004/

Clare Library online resources: https://www.clarelibrary.ie

Autumnal Rambles about New Quay - TL Cooke published in the Galway Vindicator and reprinted on the Clare Library website:

https://www.clarelibrary.ie/eolas/coclare/history/autumnal_rambles/autumnal_rambles.htm

TL Cooke was an early 19th century solicitor, historian, and collector. During his travels he made a number of trips to New Quay, where he was entertained by the gentry. His descriptions provide a rare glimpse of the state of antiquities, beliefs, and customs from a 200-year-old perspective.

1. Tale of The Skerretts of Finavarra House

Williams, V (1938). The World of Action. Hamish Hamilton.

Hardiman, J (1820). The History of the Town and County of the Town of Galway from the earliest period to the present time. Connaught Tribune 1926 (Reprint).

Prendergast, JP. (1865). The Cromwellian settlement of Ireland. Longman, Roberts, & Green.

Crossle, P. (1931). Some Records of the Skerrett Family. Journal of the Galway Archaeological Historical Society Vol. 15, No. 1/2 (1931), pp. 33-72 (40 pages)

https://www.findmypast.co.uk - Family History Website

https://www.ancestry.co.uk - Family History Website

http://www.birminghamarchdiocesanarchives.org.uk/archives_index.asp - records of Oscott students

Landed Estate records. NLI - National Library of Ireland – Manuscripts

2. The Tale of the 19th Century Poor in New Quay

Ó Gráda. Cormac. (1993). Ireland before and after the Famine: Explorations in Economic History 1800–1925. Manchester University Press.

Woodham-Smith. Cecil. (1991) [1962]. The Great Hunger: Ireland 1845–1849, London, Hamish Hamilton,

Devon Commission: Report from her Majesty's Commissioners of Inquiry into the State of the Law and Practice in Respect of the Occupation of Land in Ireland, with minutes of evidence, supplements, appendices, and index, 1845. Printed by A. Thom, for H.M.S.O., 1847.

Condition of the poorer classes in Ireland: answers to queries put to magistrates. (1838) The First Report from His Majesty's Commissioners for inquiring into the condition of the Poorer Classes in Ireland. (1835). https://catalogue.nli.ie/Record/vtls000035401

Cousens. SH. Regional Variations in Mortality During Irish Famine – Population Studies. (July 1960). Proceedings of the Royal Irish Academy Vol 63.

Irish Census Returns – Summaries 1821 to 1891. http://www.histpop.org/ohpr/servlet/Show?page=Home. UK Data Archive at the University of Essex.

Copies of Memorials addressed to the Treasury from certain Poor Law Unions in Ireland 1851. On the subject of Consolidated Annuities.

Crowley. J, Smyth. William. J, Murphy. Mike. (2012). The Atlas of the Great Irish Famine. NYU Press.

Report of the Commissioners for administering the Laws for the Relief of the Poor in England. 1848. (Second [-Twenty-Third] Annual Report of the Poor Law Board. 1849[-1870-71].). / Great Britain.

Final report from the Board of public works, Ireland, relating to measures adopted for the relief of distress in July and August 1847, with appendices / Presented to the House of Commons / Ireland.

Kennedy. L, Macraild. D.M., Darwen.L, Gurrin.B. (2022). The Death Census of Black '47: Eyewitness Accounts of Ireland's Great Famine. Anthem Press.

3. The Tale of New Quay Placenames History and Origin

Grierson, George. (1794) Statutes passed in the Parliament held in Ireland under Charles II – Vol II. Arkose Press.

Simington, R.C. (1967) Book of Survey and Distribution Vol IV County Clare 1636 – 1703 (Reproduced from manuscripts held in the Public Records Office with Introduction by R C Simington).

Ordnance Survey of Ireland Archives – Royal Irish Academy.

The history of Ordnance Survey Ireland – www.osi.ie

Joyce, P.W. (1871) The Origin and History of Irish Names of Places - (Volume 1 – 3). (2015 Classic Reprint). FB&C Limited.

Inchiquin Manuscripts. https://www.irishmanuscripts.ie/product/the-inchiquin-manuscripts/

4. The Tale of The O'Dalaigh Poets

Daly. Edmund E. (1937). History of the O'Dalys; the story of the ancient Irish sept; the race of Dalach of Corcu Adaimh. New Haven, Conn. Tuttle, Morehouse, and Taylor.

Mac Mahon. Michael. Clare's Gaelic Bardic Tradition. https://www.clarelibrary.ie/eolas/coclare/literature/bardic/bardic.htm

Spencer Edmund (1596) A view of the present state of Ireland. Published 1633.

FitzPatrick. Elizabeth (2002) Royal inauguration in Gaelic Ireland c. 1100-1600. Boydell Press; Illustrated edition.

Cooke TL Autumnal Rambles around New Quay (1842. published in Galway Vindicator and reprinted in Clare Library website.

5. The Tale of Mount Vernon Lodge

Toibin. C. (2003). Lady Gregory's toothbrush. Lilliput Press Dublin.

Gregory. Augusta. (2005) Kiltartan History Book. Dodo Press, United Kingdom.

Hill. Judith. (2011). Lady Gregory - An Irish Life. The Collins Press; Illustrated edition.

Gregory. Augusta. (1976). Lady Gregory - 70 years 1852 – 1932 Autobiography. New York Macmillan.

O Dowd, Peadar (2004) A history of County Galway; A comprehensive study of Galway's history culture and people. Gill Books.

Matteson, David Maydole. Fitzpatrick, John Clement. The writings of George Washington from the Original Manuscript Sources 1745 – 1799. Washington, U.S. Govt. Print. Off. (1931-44).

Gregory. Anne. (1978). Me and Nu: Childhood at Coole. Colin Smythe Ltd.

Pethica, James. (2009). Yeats's 'perfect man'. Dublin Review https://thedublinreview.com/product-category/archive/

6. The Tale of Sea Trade and Fishing

O'Flaherty, Roderic, 1629-1718 A Chorographical Description of West or H-Iar Connaught. Editor and translation by Hardiman, James, 1782-1855, Dublin: For the Irish Archaeological Society, 1846 https://archive.org/details/chorographicalde00ofla

Halpin. S. and O Connor. G. (2008) *Survey of quays and harbours of Clare*. Clare Coastal Architectural Heritage Survey.

Lyons M.A Maritime Relations Between Ireland and France 1480 – c1630. Irish Economic and Social History Vol. 27 (2000), pp. 1-24 (24 pages)

Cullen L.M. Five Letters Relating to Galway Smuggling in 173. Journal of the Galway archaeological and historical society Vol.27 (1956-1957).

Cullen. L. M. The Galway smuggling trade in the seventeen-thirties. Journal of the Galway archaeological and historical society Vol.30, No 1/2 (1962).

Cullen. L. M. The smuggling trade in Ireland in the eighteenth century. Proceeding of the Royal Irish Academy. Section c: Archaeology, Celtic Studies, History, Linguistics, Literature Vol. 69, (1968-1969).

Wilkins. Noel. (2017), Humble Works for Humble People: A History of the Fishery Piers of County Galway and North Clare, 1800–1922, Irish Academic Press

Villiers-Tuthill. K (2006) Alexander Nimmo & the Western District Emerging Infrastructure in Pre-Famine Ireland. Connemara Girl Publications

Hansard Parliamentary Papers - Reports of the Commissioners of Irish Fisheries

7. The Tales of Red Bank Oysters and Burton Bindon

British Newspaper Archives.

Dublin Morning Register - Monday 19 October 1829

Dublin Evening Post 1835.

Limerick Chronicle 1842

Limerick & Clare Examiner 1849

Clare Journal, and Ennis Advertiser on Thursday 26 July 1849

The Freeman's Journal - Saturday 24 September 1853.

Belfast Mercury on the 3[rd of] Jan 1855

The Tuam Herald 10th Mat 1856

MS 45,096 /2 - Inchiquin Papers Collection National Library of Ireland

Registry of Deeds Dublin – Memorial number 97454

Moriarty. Gerald. P. (2005). Dean Swift and His Writings Haskell House Publishers Inc. U.S.; New ed of 1893 ed edition (1 Feb. 1982)

Burke's Peerage

Courtenay. William. Devon Earl of. (1845) Devon Commission: Report from her Majesty's Commissioners of Inquiry into the State of the Law and Practice in Respect of the Occupation of Land in Ireland, with minutes of evidence, supplements, appendices, and index.

Some Old Irish Hunting Notes (1878) from Bailey's Magazine of Sports and Pastimes1878. London Baily Brothers (1860 – 1892).

8. The Tale of Peter Comyn

https://archive.org/details/sim_jesuit-or-catholic-sentinel_1830-08-28_1_52/page/418/mode/2up?q=comyn&view=theater
Catholic Sentinel Archives

https://www.clarelibrary.ie/eolas/coclare/history/osl/index.htm Ordnance Survey Letters by John O'Donovan and Eugene Curry

https://www.nationalarchives.ie/our-archives/explore-our-collections/collection/ Letters from the Chief Secretary's Office – Register of Papers from the National Archives

9. The Tale of Corcomroe Abbey

Cooke.TL. Autumnal Rambles about New Quay, County Clare http://www.clarelibrary.ie/eolas/coclare/history/autumnal_rambles/corcumroe_abbey.htm

McMahon. Michael. (1997). On a Fertile Rock – The Cistercian Abbey of Corcomroe. Kincora Books County Clare.

Stalley. Roger. Corcomroe Abbey, Some Observations on Its Architectural History. The Journal of the Royal Society of Antiquaries of Ireland, Vol. 105 (1975). pp. 25-46

Ní Ghabhláin. Sinéad. (1995) Church and Community in Medieval Ireland: The Diocese of Kilfenora. The Journal of the Royal Society of Antiquaries of Ireland, Vol. 125, pp. 61-84.

Nelson. E. Charles. Stalley. Roger A. (1989) Medieval Naturalism and the Botanical Carvings at Corcomroe Abbey (County Clare) Gesta, Vol. 28, No. 2, pp. 165-174

Westropp. Thomas J. (Dec. 31, 1911). Prehistoric Remains (Forts and Dolmens) in the Burren, Co. Clare. The Journal of the Royal Society of Antiquaries of Ireland, Sixth Series, Vol. 1, No. 4. pp. 343-360.

Mac Ruaidhrí Mac Craith (translated by Standish Hayes O'Grady 1929) Caithréim Thoirdhealbhaigh (War of the Turloughs) 2 vols, Irish Texts Society, 26, 27, London: Irish Texts Society.

Yeats. William. Butler. (1919). The dreaming of the bones - Cornell University Press edition (2003)

O' Clery. Lughdaigh. (1895) The Life of Hugh Roe O'Donnell. Beatha Aodha Ruaidh Ui Domhnaill. Prince of Tirconnell, (1586-1602). First Published from Cucogry O'Clery's Irish Manuscript in the R.I. A., with Historical, Introduction, Translation, Notes, and Illustrations by Rev. Denis Murphy. Dublin: Fallon.

O' Conbhuidhe. Colmcille. (1998) Studies in Irish Cistercian history edited by Finbarr Donovan. Four Courts Press.

Orpen. Goddard H. (April 1913) Some Irish Cistercian Documents: The English Historical Review: Vol. 28, No. 110. pp. 303-313 (11 pages) Published By: Oxford University Press

O'Donoghue. John (1999) Anam Cara: Spiritual Wisdom from the Celtic World. Bantam Press.

10. The Tale of Oughtmama Monastery

Fahey, Jerome. M. H. (1893). The History and Antiquities of the Diocese of Kilmacduagh. M. H. Gill & son,

Grattan-Flood. William. St. Colman. (1908). The Catholic Encyclopaedia. Vol. 4. New York. Robert Appleton Company.

Gibson. D. Blair. (2012) From Chiefdom to State in Early Ireland. Cambridge University Press; Illustrated edition.

Ní Ghabhlain. Sinéad. (1996). The Origin of Medieval Parishes in Gaelic Ireland: The Evidence from Kilfenora. The Journal of the Royal Society of Antiquaries of Ireland, Vol. 126 pp. 37-61 (25 pages). Published By: Royal Society of Antiquaries of Ireland

Map of Abbey and Oughtmama townlands:
https://www.clarelibrary.ie/eolas/coclare/places/oughtmana_townlands.htm

Ní Ghabhláin. Sinead. (1995). Church, parish and policy, the medieval diocese of Kilfenora Ireland. Unpublished PHD thesis.

Gray. Richard. (2006). Settlement clusters at parish churches in Ireland. c. 1200-1600 AD. PHD thesis.
http://hdl.handle.net/10379/6061 NUIG

Dunraven. Earl of. (1875 and 1877). Notes on Irish Architecture, Volume 1 & 2. London: George Bell & Sons.

O Donovan. John. (1864). The Martyrology of Donegal; A calendar of the Saints of Ireland. Notes: The Martyrology of Donegal was written by Mícheál Ó Cléirigh (1590-1643) in the 17th century and edited and translated by John O'Donovan in 1864. The martyrology is based on a series of earlier documents which recorded the saints of Donegal, their feast days, and biographical details.

Frost. James. (1893). The History and Topography of the County of Clare. Sealey Bryers and Walker Dublin 1893.

Stokes. Whitley. (2018). The Tripartite Life of Patrick: With Other Documents Relating to that Saint Vol.I. Creative Media Publications.

Keating. Geoffrey. (1634). History of Ireland, Vita Sti Colmani, Life of the Saints. Translated by John O Mahony. Irish Roots Café.

11. The Tale of Saint Patrick's Well

Kirby. Tony. and Geh. Nick. (2020). Etching Memories at a Holy Well. https://www.heartofburrenwalks.com/etch-ing-memories-at-a-holy-well

Archdall. Mervyn. (1786). Monasticon Hibernicum. Gale ECCO, Print Editions (2018)

12. The Tale of Turlough Hill

Westropp. Thomas. Johnson. (1911). *Prehistoric Forts and Dolmens in North Clare*. Part IV: The Eastern Border. Turlough Hill. Journal of the Royal Historical and Archaeological Association of Ireland.

Clare Library Website: https://www.clarelibrary.ie/eolas/coclare/archaeology/arch_burren/part4_eastern_border_turlough_hill.htm

Mystery surrounds Burren settlement excavated by archaeologists. (April 2016).
https://www.irishtimes.com/news/ireland/irish-news/mystery-surrounds-burren-settlement-excavated-by-archaeologists-1.2629951

Bergh. Stefan Dr. *Surveying Turlough Hill.* Dr Stefan Bergh
https://www.universityofgalway.ie/colleges-and-schools/arts-social-sciences-and-celtic-studies/geography-archaeology-irish-studies/disciplines/archaeology/research/ireland-atlantic-europe/surveying- turlough-hill/

Milton Keynes UK
Ingram Content Group UK Ltd.
UKHW042353140124
436045UK00003B/18